$\mathscr{D}$edication

To the four children: Steve, Tim, Theo, and Dolley; and to Brother Willard Collins and Ruth; and to Margaret Roberts, who spent many tireless hours spelling the words right and checking scriptures, and who was an invaluable help in putting this together.

Marching to Zion

Ira North

Gospel Advocate Company

Cover design by Gregory A. Needels. Book design by Susan A. Barnes.

Unless otherwise indicated, Scripture quotations are from the King James Version.

Published by Christian Communications,
a division of the Gospel Advocate Company
PO Box 150, Nashville, TN 37202

ISBN 0-89225-454-8

Table of Contents

Ira North:
Man of Compassion

Foreword by Avon North

He has been called flamboyant, a show-off, "Fiery Irey," Mr. Enthusiasm, a liberal, the great North star from the east, and many other names — some complimentary and some not so complimentary. To me the real Ira can best be described as a "Man of Compassion" — a lover of the very young, the very old, the poor, the downtrodden and the little homeless children.

There is no better way to train up a child than by example. Ira was born into a poor but compassionate family. Though they were poor, his parents were always willing to share with those less fortunate. Even after their financial situation was much better, they still held to this attitude.

When Ira was about 4 years old, his paternal grandfather became unable to live alone and care for himself. There were no nursing homes at that time. Believing strongly in the saying that "an old tree cannot survive being transplanted into fresh soil, it would soon wither and die," the family did not move him from his home but moved in with him. He was a beloved old preacher of 50 years.

His four-year-old grandson, Ira, loved to sit on his knee and hear him tell how wonderful it was to preach the Gospel. The desire was instilled in this young boy to preach the Gospel. It stayed with him all of his life, until his death at age 62.

Soon after the death of his grandfather, Ira's maternal grandmother became unable to care for herself. The Norths again moved their family, this time to the grandmother's home. Every morning she would have Ira get in bed with her and rub her back. She said that he was the best back-rubber in the world. These were precious memories, and Ira never lost his love and compassion for the elderly.

At the time Ira started to school, Lawrence County, Tennessee, had a "poor farm". It was a place provided for the poorest of the poor, supported by the county. The children from the county poor farm attended the same school as Ira. The school had no cafeteria, and all the kids carried their lunch to school. Soon after Ira started to school, his mother realized that Ira wasn't eating his lunch. He was giving it to the county poor farm kids. No, she didn't fuss at him. She just fixed more food each day for him to share.

During college days, Ira shared his suits with a preacher friend who didn't have clothes to wear to preach. One incident happened in Baton Rouge during graduate school. I was in the hospital with a new baby. I had stored in enough food to provide for Ira and my two little boys until Grandma could get there, but I had not provided for the hungry stranger who came by. Yes, Ira gave him the last quart of milk in the refrigerator, not even thinking that his own little boys might get hungry before morning. Needless to say, they survived, and Grandma came the next day.

So we came to our preaching years at Madison. I truly believe that God had a plan for a great demonstration to be established that would be an example for the church everywhere to follow. I believe that He selected the right location, the right leadership, the right people, and He raised up the right preacher to lead them and help to make it all happen. It seems to me that Ira was being prepared for this work since he was a very young child.

Always in the back of Ira's mind was a complete facility for the homeless, aged and poor. One Sunday morning, early in his ministry at Madison, he called a little 8-year-old boy to the stage to stand with him. He announced to the audience, "This is Eddie. He is going to the reform school tomorrow. He hasn't broken any law. His only problem is that nobody wants him and the only place that he can go is to a correction institution." Ira noticed an older man in the audience whisper something to his wife, and she nodded her head. Then the man raised his hand and said, "Look no further, Brother North. Birdie and I will give Eddie a home until Madison can build one." Ira said, "God bless you, Brother Perry and Birdie. You now have you a boy." Later Birdie related to us that the first night when she tucked him into bed, the little boy said, "I ain't had no mama to kiss me good night." Eddie was our first child in our child care demonstration, which surpassed 1,000 several years ago. So Madison was in the child care business. One of Ira's dreams came true.

About the time that little Eddie appeared on the scene, Madison was practically given a 42-acre plot of land located about one mile from the church building. Eventually seven cottages were built for neglected children; a retirement village with 24 private apartments for the aged; and just before he died, Ira shoveled the first shovel of dirt to break the ground for a new villa for people who can no longer cook and keep an apartment. This facility cares for 24 people. Ira's dream of a lifetime come true. The child care cottages are called Happy Acres. The apartment complex is called the Golden Age Village, and the villa is called the Christian Care Villa.

"Mister, is this the church what helps people?" Ira quickly replied, "Well, I'll declare! There are 750 churches in this town, and you have found the right one."

During his ministry Madison pioneered cottage-type homes for children. Each nice four-bedroom brick home is located on a two-acre lot. The cottages house a mama, a daddy and six children. To make it as near to a normal home as possible, the dad works for a living and the mom cares for the home and children. This plan for child care was acclaimed by the state welfare department. The welfare department could furnish a child's physical needs, but it could not give a child the warm compassionate love and care that we could with our plan.

By 1973 there were over 60 homes like this supported by churches of Christ. This program has grown to include an adoption agency, foster home care, and a home for abused wives with three social workers, a full-time family life counselor, and a student intern working on an advanced degree in social work. A collection taken in the Bible school classes each Sunday is the only source of support for this program. May God forgive us if we have misused any gifts that we have had at our disposal.

Ira frequently related the incident about the "Church What Helps People." One afternoon he was in the office after everybody else was gone. There was a timid knock at his outside door. He went to the door, and there stood two frightened little girls. "Mister, is this the church what helps people?" Ira quickly replied, "Well, I'll declare! There are 750 churches in this town, and you have found the right one. What can I do for you?" "Our Daddy's sick and we are hungry," they answered. "Well, we'll fix that. Come with me." He took them to the food room and found the door locked. "Well, what do you know? Somebody forgot and locked the door." He picked up a hammer and broke the lock and sent the little girls home with their arms filled with sacks of food. Before leaving them he invited them to Bible school the next Sunday.

Ira's concern for the people in the slums of the inner city was reflected in the following quote from a sermon: "What have the religious people, what have the churches done for the poor of the inner city?

What has Christendom done? I'll tell you what we have done. For all practical purposes nothing. When the poor move in, we move out. We don't want to get our hands dirty. They live in unspeakable poverty in some cases. Oh, how those little children need to know about Jesus! How they need to feel the hand of someone clean who cares. What have we done? We've moved out and we've worshiped in our big, fine buildings with wall-to-wall carpets and air conditioners and ridden in our nice cars and lived in our nice homes and wrung our hands and said, 'Oh, those terrible people down in the slums.' We haven't lifted a finger to help them."

Ira did do something to help them. He was instrumental in getting the Nashville Inner City Ministry started. He helped obtain permission to use one of the inner-city school auditoriums each Sunday morning for worship. There are about 400 people who worship there each Sunday. They now own a fleet of 42 busses and take 1,200 people each Monday and Tuesday nights to area churches for a Bible class. They have seven people who work full-time and hundreds of volunteers. This ministry is an example. It is training people from other cities to begin a ministry in their own area. There are eight young men going to Lipscomb on a scholarship from a fund established in honor of Marshall Keeble. The inner city is marching, and I feel that Ira's early encouragement has helped to bring this about.

Even on his deathbed Ira was thinking of and concerned about the little children. He had received so many notes and get well wishes from little children who assured him that they prayed for him at every meal and at bedtime. He was concerned that they might think that God didn't answer their prayers. So he requested that Jim Bill McInteer explain to the little children at the funeral that God answers our prayers His way and not our way.

When Ira died, I lost my best friend, but it was wonderful to share 43 years, four children and 11 grandchildren with such a friend!

Avon North

The Church Centered Around the Cross

"God forbid that I should glory, save in the cross of our Lord Jesus Christ" (Galatians 6:14). The Christian religion centers around the Cross. In our lesson today I'd like to point out from the Bible several ways in which this is true.

The church centers around the Cross. The Bible teaches us in Acts 20:28 that Christ purchased the church with His own blood: "Feed the church of God, which he hath purchased with his own blood." The blood of Jesus is in the church of our Lord. The Bible says in Ephesians 1:22-23 that Christ Jesus is the head and the church is the body. The head of the church died on the cross. The message that is preached by the church is the message of the cross; the good news that comes from the cross. First Timothy 3:15 says, "If I tarry long, that thou mayest know how thou oughtest to behave thyself in the house of God, which is the church of the living God,

the pillar and ground of the truth." The support of
the preaching of the Gospel is the duty of the church
of our Lord. So the church centers around the Cross.

Second, we need to remember that redemption centers around the Cross. John said in 1 John 1:7, "If we
walk in the light, as he is in the light, we have fellowship one with another, and the blood of Jesus Christ
his Son cleanseth us from all sin." Jesus shed His
blood in His death, and we come in contact with it
through the death of our blessed Lord when we are
baptized into His death (Romans 6:3-4). It is there
that we meet the blood of Jesus and it is there that
blood takes away our sins. In Acts 22:16 we read
what happens when Saul of Tarsus, who has persecuted the Church, becomes penitent and realizes he is
lost: "And now why tarriest thou? arise, and be baptized, and wash away thy sins, calling on the name of
the Lord." Redemption centers around the Cross.

Third, we need to bear in mind that the observance
of the Lord's Supper centers around the Cross. It is
interesting that our Lord didn't command us to put
a cross up on every corner. Some people climb the
mountaintops and set up a big cross, and I'm not
fighting that, but the Bible teaches us to observe the
Lord's Supper on the first day of the week (Acts
20:7). The Lord's Supper centers around the Cross.
If we partake of it in a worthy manner, with respect,
the Cross is always in our mind. I have people say to
me, "I don't feel I'm good enough to take the Lord's
Supper." I don't either, and anybody who does is a
self-righteous hypocrite. People who feel worthy
don't understand the Cross. They don't understand
that we cannot merit our salvation. We are depend-

ing not on our own goodness but on the goodness of Jesus Christ. We examine ourselves and are careful to observe the Supper in a respectful manner, in a reverent manner, in a manner becoming a memorial to our Lord and Savior Jesus Christ. Without the Cross we couldn't do that.

The separation of God's covenants centers around the Cross. The old Law of Moses was in effect until the Cross, but it was nailed to the cross (Colossians 2:14). We speak of the New Testament meaning the new will. It was not in effect until Jesus died on the cross. It is important to understand that.

Someone asks, "Why do we not have the burning of incense in the worship service? They had it under the Mosaic law. Why is it we do not have the lighting of lamps? Why is it we do not have the mechanical instruments of music? Why is it we do not have the literal offering of animal sacrifices as commanded and practiced under the Law of Moses? Why is it we do not worship on Saturday and keep Saturday? It was commanded in the Law of Moses. Why can't a man have a thousand wives if he wants them? They certainly had a multiplicity of wives under the Law of Moses."

Yes, they did all of those things. But the lighting of lamps, burning of incense, use of mechanical instruments of music, keeping of Saturday in worship, and practice of polygamy belong to a different age, to a different covenant, to the Law of Moses. Paul says that old law was a schoolmaster to bring us to Christ, and it was nailed to the Cross.

"A man's will is not in effect until he dies," the writer of the Hebrew letter says. Everybody ought to have a will. It was difficult for me to get my father to make a will. He said, "There isn't any need in it." I said, "Oh yes there is. Everybody ought to have a will, and if you don't make one, the state of Tennessee makes one for you." Remember this about a will: it is in effect only when the testator, the man who makes it, dies.

When I was a young preacher in Baton Rouge, Louisiana, I met the most cantankerous old woman I ever saw. She had left everything she had to the church in a will. And she told the church, "You take care of me until I die, and I will leave you everything in my will." Well I went to see her. My wife and I had not been in her house three minutes before she started telling me how mean and unthoughtful the ladies were at the church of Christ.

I remember coming out and going by to see my friend Dolph Bryant, who was in the English department at LSU. I said, "Brother Bryant, how long have you known Sister So-n-So? He said, "All my life." I said, "How was she when she was young?" He said, "Just like she is now. She was cantankerous and ugly and mean." That gave rise to the coining of a phrase that when you get old, "you is what you is only a little more 'iser." When you are mean and ugly as a young person, you are a bear cat when you get old. Age throws off restraint. If you are sweet and kind and good, then you get sweeter and kinder and better.

Do you know what this lady did? She got mad at the church one day and changed her will. When the woman died, the church that had spent years and thousands of dollars on her didn't get a cotton-pickin' penny! Don't get the big head and don't get all excited when somebody says, "I remembered you in my will." Until the testator dies, the will is not in effect and it might be changed a dozen times.

The preaching of the Cross is the power of God unto salvation.

The writer of the Hebrew letter says that the will is not in effect until the testator dies. When our blessed Lord died on the cross, then the old law was nailed to that cross, taken out of the way, and we were given a New Covenant, a new law. The separation of God's covenants centers around the Cross.

Salvation centers around the Cross. First Corinthians 15:3 says that Jesus died for our sins. The Jews offered the literal ram sacrifice. But Jesus left the shining courts of heaven, was born in a barn, lived among men, and died for our sins. He is the lamb of God that takes away the sins of the world (John 1:29). The preaching of the Cross is the power of God unto salvation. The preaching of the Cross is foolishness to them that perish, but to us who believe, it is power of God unto salvation. Man becomes free from sin when he obeys from the heart that form of doctrine (Romans 6:17-18).

When does a man become free of sin? Reminds me of a question I have often been asked by young people: "When are a man and a woman married in the sight of God?" It grieves me that there are preachers who do not know. There are Sunday school teachers who do not know. Some of these young people are utterly confused. They don't know when a man and a woman are married. I'll tell you when they are married. When they go down and buy the license? Not yet! When they come up before the preacher? Not yet! When they say, "I do," and the preacher says, "By the authority invested in me as a minister of the Gospel by the great state of Tennessee, I now pronounce you husband and wife"? That is it! Right there! That's it! That very second! They are now married in the sight of the state! They are now married in the sight of Mama! They are married in the sight of Papa! They are married in the sight of the elders! They are married in the sight of the preacher! They are married in the sight of the neighbors! That moment!

I remember marrying a big old tall boy, and when I said, "I now pronounce you husband and wife," I thought he was going to faint. I asked him later, "Son, what shook you up?" He said, "When you said 'by the authority invested in me as a minister of the Gospel in the great state of Tennessee I now pronounce you husband and wife' I felt like I had been shot by a cannon. I'll never forget that moment." I said, "I hope you don't as long as you live."

I can tell you when you are cleansed from sin. The Bible gives the answer in Romans 6:17-18. A man came over to my office this week to be baptized. We waded out into the water. I said, "Do you believe with all of your heart that Jesus Christ is the Son of God?" He said, "I do believe with all of my heart." Not yet are the sins gone! Yes, he was penitent. I could tell that. He could hardly choke back the tears. Then I raised my hand and said, "Upon the confession of your faith in our Lord and Savior Jesus Christ and for the remission of your sins, I now baptize you into the name of the Father, the Son and the Holy Spirit. Amen!" And I buried him in baptism, and he came forth a new creature. He believed in Jesus; he died to sin; he was buried; and he was raised to walk in newness of life. Paul said that having obeyed from the heart that form of doctrine — the death, burial and resurrection — he is then made free from sin (Romans 6:17). That is the moment we meet the death of Christ; we meet His blood and we are cleansed from sin. Not by the water, not by our own merit, but by the blessed blood of Jesus. Paul says the blood of bulls and goats could not take away sins. All those sacrifices before our blessed Lord died on the cross in a sense were rolling the people's sins forward until the blood of Jesus. The blood of Jesus worked both ways. It took care of the sins of those who lived under that old law, and it takes care of our sins today. Yes, salvation is centered around the cross of Christ.

You know a lot of our brethren don't understand that Sunday school ... benevolent work ... mission work ... is soul winning.

Last, let us remember our text, "God forbid that I should glory, save in the cross of our Lord Jesus Christ." A few years ago Brother Willard Collins came to me and said, "It is time for you to write a book." I said, "Willard, I'm trying to hold down two jobs and have four children. What are you talking about?" He said, "You know God has been good to you and that church out at Madison, and you need to share it." So I wrote a little book called *Marching for the Master*. On the front cover Brother Paul Moore, who is a genius in this matter of designing, fixed a man marching. I went to Brother Goodpasture and said, "Brother Goodpasture, I need some help. I'm worried about this book. You know a lot of our brethren don't understand that Sunday school is soul winning. A lot of them don't understand that benevolent work is soul winning. A lot of them don't understand mission work is soul winning. The reason we are interested in the Sunday school and the reason we are interested in benevolence and the reason we are interested in mission work and the reason we want a church to march is because we believe in Jesus. We believe in His life, His death, His burial, His resurrection. Suggest something I can put on the front of this book that will help to suggest that." He said, "Well, I would suggest Galatians 6:14." So under the man marching he wrote: "God forbid that I should glory save in the cross of Christ."

The cross of Christ is our message, our hope, our security.

The Cross shows us in its special way the justice of God. The Cross shows in a special way the love of God. The Cross shows the perfect harmony of the justice and the love of God. Justice for sin in that the Son of God died. Love in that He gave His life for you and me while we were yet sinners. The cross of Christ is our security. Ladies and gentlemen, there is no security in this world except the cross of Christ. It is not in worldly wisdom; it is not in riches; it is not in honor; it doesn't make any difference how much money you have for it takes just one bad deal to sink you if the deal is big enough.

I knew George Pepperdine well. He founded Western Auto and made millions. He endowed Pepperdine University, but one day he made a housing deal. It was a big one. He went broke. He lost his fortune. I can remember thinking when I saw that old gray-headed man broke, "What a blessing it was that he did something with his money while he could."

There is no security in worldly wisdom or worldly riches or worldly honor. The only true security is in the cross of Christ. The cross of Christ is our hope. If you are trusting in your own self-righteousness, in your own goodness, what a sad disappointment is going to come. The cross of Christ is our message, our hope, our security.

"When I survey the wondrous cross on which the Prince of Glory died, my richest gain I count but loss and pour contempt on all my pride."

Let us bow and pray: Oh, Lord God of Heaven, we pray that You will teach us today to glory in the cross of Christ. We thank You, our Father, for the glorious privilege of being members of that heaven-born, blood-bought institution, the church. We thank You for our redemption. We thank You, our Father, that we can observe the Lord's Supper and remember the cross. We are thankful, Father, that salvation can be ours, not by our own goodness and righteousness but by the cross of Christ. Our Father, if we have gloried in our life at any time in anything other than in the cross of Christ, would You please forgive us? And would You help us all to live within the shadow of the Cross? If there is one precious soul who has never obeyed from the heart that form of doctrine, we pray that they will want to come, confess Jesus and be baptized today for we ask it in the name of Jesus the Christ. Amen.

∽

Madison Church of Christ
Nashville, Tennessee
August 14, 1974, a.m.

Is the Church Relevant Today?

I have a message on my heart as big as Lookout Mountain. I pray that I will be able to transfer it to your heart. I pray that I can say something that will encourage you and send you home ready to work for the Master. I want to talk about the relevancy of the church in changing times.

My friends, I can understand why there are some questioning the relevance of the church today. We haven't always set a good example. But the church could and should be relevant and always will be. The church is a place of worship and, after all, God made us a worshiping people. We need to meet together, pray together, partake of the Lord's Supper together, sing together, be together.

I hear people say occasionally, "I believe I can worship at home just as well and stay home and read the Bible." Well, that is not what God thinks and that is not what the Christian says. The Bible says in Hebrews 10:25: "Not forsaking the assembling of ourselves together, as the manner of some is; but exhorting one another: and so much more, as ye see the day approaching ."

I used to go hunting in Middle Tennessee near an old church building. I asked how often they met and someone answered, "Once a month." A few years later I was rabbit hunting there and said, "How often does this church meet?" Someone answered, "Once a year." I said, "Well, that is as close to the Bible as once a month." They are both missing it. The Bible teaches we are to meet on the first day of the week — not once a month, not once a year. The last time I was quail hunting, someone had turned the building into a barn. The church had completely died.

We need to worship God. Worship is an emotion to pour out our souls in adoration. I hear people say, "I didn't get much out of the service." Well, maybe that is the problem. Some people are coming to *get*. When I attend services, I go to *give* my heart, my love, my money, my moral support, my loyalty — to pour out my heart in adoration to worship the God Almighty. The church will always be relevant for that reason — we need a place to give worship to God.

The church as it could be and should be is a place of work. I can understand how sometimes a youngster will go by an expensive building and ask, "How often is this building used?" "Three hours a week." "You mean with all these millions invested in sticks and stones, brick and mortar, it is only used three hours a week? When there are homeless children and poor people and the lowly and a thousand things that need to be done, all this money is tied up in bricks and mortar?" No, I'm not defending buildings that are not used. They need to be places of work for God. "I must work the works of him that sent me, while it is day: [for] the night cometh, when no man can work" (John 9:4).

The Lord does not require greatness, just service.

I can go by a church building on Monday, Tuesday, Wednesday, Thursday or Friday, and I can just about tell you the temperature of that congregation. You show me a building that is just like a beehive on Monday, Tuesday, Wednesday, Thursday and Friday and I'll show you a church not only that is relevant, but I'll show you a church that the devil and all the angels of hell, plus the U.S. Marine Corps, cannot keep from marching and growing. It is a thrilling thing for me when I go by a church building during the week and I see a lot of activity. But when you pass a building and maybe you can find one secretary, it is a dead museum. I tell you, it is not going to grow very much.

The church could be and should be a place of serving: "But he that is greatest among you shall be your servant" (Matthew 23:11). Remember in John 13 when the Lord took the towel and basin and washed the disciples' feet, the question of greatness never came up. The Lord does not require greatness, just service. After that great lesson as far as I know, the question never again came up as to who is the greatest.

Ladies and gentlemen, never in the history of the world have there been such tremendous opportunities

to be of service. If we as a church put up a big museum and put our money in sticks and stones, I can
understand why the world is going to shake its head
and say, "This does not belong to our age and time."

There a thousand ways to a good Christian life.
I'd like to mention a few to you. There are about
two million unwanted, uncared for, abused children
in the United States of America. Two million. Do
you know what we do many times? We just do a lot
of preaching on pure and undefiled religion. It
would take the Pacific Ocean to hold all our preaching, but I could put all our practice in a little
Middle Tennessee pond — or as they say out in
West Texas, that wonderful God-forsaken country,
"in a little tank." I'll tell you one thing — if preaching alone would get it done, we would already have
the world.

Everybody back home knows we can out-preach
them all — out-preach them, out-quote them, out-
debate them, skin them, and tack their hides to the
wall. They also know that is just talk. When it
comes to practice, a little Civitan club that meets in
a downtown hotel room can out-do us in the same
capacity. But, wonderful, unbelievable and glorious
things happen to a church that gets all excited about
ministering to the poor and the lowly and the homeless and the aged and the down-trodden — that
begins to practice a little bit.

I have seen it with my own eyes. We have a little
better than one addition a day at Madison. In fact,
we had an average of almost one and a half a day
last year. Now I'll have to say that this response is
not because of the preaching. It is not based on the

invitations. Do you know how many invitation songs we sing? One, and sometimes we sing just one or two verses. If you are going to be baptized at the Madison Church of Christ, you better make up your mind and get down that aisle, boy, and quick. I'm not criticizing churches that sing on and on and on. I'm just saying when the church is a place of service, the heart is open, and the teaching program is active, the problem is getting them to wait until they are old enough to understand to be baptized.

I want to tell you about another little work I have seen in service that comes from a very simple little thing, yet a wonderful thing. You know there are a lot of people who are old and not able either physically or financially to have one good, hot meal a day. We put up a building and we teach, teach, teach. Yet there are people in the community who are old and sick and are unable to have one good balanced meal a day in the shadow of that new building.

So at Madison we started a program last year called Meals on Wheels. We called the Metropolitan health nurse and asked her to give us names of people who were old and unable to have one balanced meal a day. Two ladies volunteer to plan the menu and do the cooking for a week at a time. Their week comes around about once a year. The homes of the needy are divided into five routes. Two ladies volunteer to deliver one day a week for each route. Since the same two ladies deliver the same route every week they can get acquainted with the people on their route and help them in other ways. We always have two women ride together because the neighborhoods they go into are sometimes unsafe for a woman to go alone. Last year we served over 9,000 meals at the cost of 32 cents a meal. This was possible because so much food and money were donated. When you get involved in a project like this, everybody wants to give you money. It is a wonderful thing.

You know, when you get involved in helping the poor, I guarantee you the young people can see and want to help.

Mrs. North is in charge of this program. Last winter when we had a cold, icy, snowy day, she came into my office and announced, "We are not going to miss today because of the ice and snow." Many of our women were not comfortable driving on the ice, so I asked, "Who is going to deliver?" She said, "You!" I said, "Well, all right." So we got in the little pickup truck and did the delivering. In every home we went into, people would say, "Brother North, talk to us awhile." Some would say, "Brother North, please pray for us before you leave." Talk about something that warms your heart.

I remember when a couple of young married ladies came by my office one day and said, "Brother North, we have a story for you. We have just taken a meal to a blind man about 80 years old. We knocked on the door and told him we were from the Madison Church of Christ and that someone would bring him a hot meal every day at noon. He said, 'I got a fork back there somewhere in the kitchen.' We said, 'We'll get it for you.' We went to the kitchen and found a fork with peanut butter on it, washed it, and brought it to him. He broke down and cried. Brother North, we don't know why, but we cried too."

Do you know what else they said to me? "We don't know how much good this will do him, but we know that we will never be the same." Oh, the opportunities for service! You know, when you get involved in helping the poor, I guarantee you the young people can see and want to help.

Now let's talk about another way you can serve: Mother's Day Out. We say to every mother in the community, "You can have one day you can call your own because we are going to take care of your children and teach them the Bible. We will start at 7:30 and let them go when school is out."

A young mother was in my office one day not long ago. While I am not a psychiatrist, I had enough graduate work in psychology to know when a person is on the verge of a nervous breakdown, and she was there. She and her husband were fussing like cats and dogs. I asked her, "How long have you been married?" She said, "Four years." I said, "How many children do you have?" She said, "Just four, but you know I'm expecting another one in a few months." I said, "You do have one day a week to call your own, don't you?" She said, "On my husband's salary? I haven't had a day off since we married." I said, "Well, you are going to have a day off or you may be out here in the insane asylum."

I have a little knowledge of that problem. I said to my wife one time when all four of our children were home. "Man, you got it made. You get to stay here all day with these precious, darling little ones." She said, "I'll tell you what, brother. I'll trade places with you tomorrow." I said, "That will be fine." Well, she left out too early, about seven in the morning. Steve turned over a gallon of molasses at the top of the stairs. Tim spilled his milk. Dolley got jelly all over everything. Before my wife left, she had told me to clean the kitchen and scrub the bathroom. When she finally came in that night, I was fit to be tied. I said, "Sweetheart, don't ever do this to me again! I'd rather hold 10 meetings all across the country than be cooped up with these bawling, squalling young'uns all day long. Don't you ever do this to me again!" I've got respect for mothers.

Now, what do you think that young mother I talked about a minute ago needed? Did she need a lot of preaching? Did she need a lot of lecturing? No! What she needed was for somebody to say to her, "Look, we care about your home and we care about you."

When I recommended this Mother's Day Our program, one brother said, "Now wait a minute. We don't have a cafeteria." I said, "We didn't have a cafeteria at Ethridge, either but I carried my lunch in a paper poke [sack]. It didn't hurt me." Then another one said, "Those kids need to go to bed. We don't have any beds." I said, "We didn't have beds at Ethridge either, but we had company. We just put a pallet on the floor, and we had fun." Then the elders gave the wonderful response that we hear so often in Tennessee, "We don't have any money." I said, "That is all right. We will charge mothers a dollar per child if they can pay and no charge if they can't pay." Brother Lillie said, "Do you mean we are going to get all that Bible taught without a penny from the church treasury?" I said, "That is right." He said, "That is wonderful. Let it roll."

To make a long story short, I wish you could see the building on Thursdays when those mothers come, some of them with one child in this arm, one on this hand, and dragging one behind her. Then see them come when the day is over with their hair fixed and fresh and pretty.

One day I was preaching at Madison, and I said, "When you get married, get up in the morning, comb your hair, and come to the breakfast table looking like a human being. I can understand why some men are having problems because they have breakfast with a rag mop. Their wife slops around the kitchen in a Hoover apron. Then after they have been at work all day and come home, what meets them at the door? A drowned rat — hair all pinned up and hasn't had a bath all day! There is one thing you can say about the women at the office: They don't look like drowned rats. They don't look like rag mops. They are clean and neat, and they smell good! That is how it ought to be at home.

I don't care how sloppy you get all day. When 5 o'clock comes, be clean, be neat. And when he gets home, meet him at the door, grab him, and send chills up and down his spine like a window shade. I tell you one thing: When the old boy's mind wanders, there is just one way it will wander and that is back home to you.

A little woman met me at the door, and she really preached my funeral. She said, "Yeah, be neat, be clean, smell good. How in the name of common sense can you do that when you are cooped up all day with four bawling, squalling young'uns?" Well, I said, "We've got the answer to that. You know our Mother's Day Out was such a success on Thursdays that we now have it on Tuesdays and Fridays too. We have three Bible kindergartens. One runs a half day, one runs all day, and one runs the other half of the day. On Saturday we take the underprivileged children in the neighborhood and have a Saturday day camp where we feed them a good meal and teach them about Jesus. If a church like this isn't relevant, then "God didn't make little green apples and it don't rain in Indianapolis in the summertime." The church as it could be and should be is a place of service.

Last, what the church could be and should be is a place of fellowship. First John 1:7 reads: "If we walk in the light, as he is in the light, we have fellowship one with another, and the blood of Jesus Christ his Son cleanseth us from all sin." Right along with being saved is fellowship. How wonderful! Thank God there is one place on this earth where I'm accepted and loved, not for what I have but for what I am. I've got news for you — in the church of Christ it doesn't make any difference whether you have $10 million or you don't have a dime; you are a brother in Christ. We have got to make sure we act that way.

I was in Boston a few weeks ago and down in the heart of that great city I saw a big, fine building nailed up. Do you know what happened? The same thing that happened in Nashville, Tennessee, and every other major city in this country. When the poor, lowly and humble move in, we freeze them out with our mink stoles and our white gloves and our big cars. We let it be known that they are not loved, accepted or wanted. We hold out until we are completely surrounded. Then we move out to the fashionable rich suburbs. I can understand that when that happens people in their homes say, "Does the church really belong in our day and age?"

The church as it could and should be is not only relevant, but it is the most wonderful and glorious thing on this planet we call earth.

I made a speech at David Lipscomb College a few months ago and I told them, "I'll tell you one thing. We ain't going to run. We have white Bible school teachers and we have black, and we have people in that congregation can't read or write their name sitting right beside a man with a Ph.D. in biochemistry. We have people who have mink and people who that don't even wear a coat, but we are all one. We are not offended or offensive. We ain't going to run! We are going to take a stand. We are going to love everybody, and we are going to accept everybody. And we are going to open our hearts and our homes to everybody who breathes, so help us God." If a church like that is not relevant in our day, then there isn't any oil in Texas, no gold in Kentucky, no country music in Tennessee, and no mosquitoes in Florida.

The church as it could and should be is not only relevant, but it is the most wonderful and glorious thing on this planet we call earth. Yes, it is! Sometimes I am asked, "When will the time come when we write off the church? When will the time come when we can really go back to the dark ages?" If you are talking

about the church we read about in the Bible, I'm
going to answer that question tonight. I'm going to
tell you when you can write it off. I'm going to tell you
when you can just say, "It is gone; it is irrelevant."

All right, are you ready? You can write it off when
the sun comes up in the West and when Ira North
dresses like he is presiding over a funeral home and
when he is the bearer of bad news, then, my brother,
you can write off the church. In case you missed my
point, let me make it clear — never.

But until that day comes, let God be made true
and every man a liar: The church will endure, and
the gates of hell will not prevail against it. Yes, I
love the church. I know it is the uplifting of the
called out. Because I know that we are human, that
sometimes I see in us prejudice and self-righteousness, in that day I see myself naked and miserable
and vulnerable. I want to plead for the grace of God.
I love the church for what it could be and what it
should be, and I'm going to be in there pitching for it
from now on. Yes, I know there is suffering and pain
in family life. I know sometimes there is not a dime
ahead and sometimes it seems that when we can see
daylight, a baby comes up with measles or worse.
I'm going to tell you one thing: The church is the
grandest and the greatest and the finest arrange-
ment ever known to mortal man. It is relevant today
and tomorrow and tomorrow and tomorrow.

∾

Pepperdine Lectures
Malibu, California
May, 1965

What is Right
with the Church?

We hear a lot of talk in our day and age about what is wrong with the church. I want to speak this morning on "What is right with the church?"

But first I want to talk about our country. We hear a lot of talk about what is wrong with our country. There is a lot wrong with our country. I'm grieved over the smut and filth and pornography that floods this country. The Supreme Court of this country did a tremendous disservice, in my humble judgement, when it opened up floodgates for every vile and ugly thing man wants to print. I went in the little drugstore across the street the other day, and I was just embarrassed. It was filled with girlie magazines and boys 14, 15 and 16 standing around thumbing through them. I couldn't help but think that this is a pretty poor foundation for building great families, families based on love and respect. This is a poor foundation for teaching the beauty and loveliness and dignity and sweetness and fineness of Christian womanhood.

There is a lot wrong with this country. It is tragic that so much of our effort should be devoted to destruction. I could spend a lot of time criticizing the United States, but I stood with Gen. Hugh Mott yesterday in the national cemetery right up the street. On Memorial Day, in that hallowed spot, surrounded by thousands of little white markers with little American flags dotting the graves of brave men, I said, "My, what a great country. There is so much right with this country." The commander of the American Legion of the State of Tennessee, a fine young lawyer from Columbia, gave the talk. He pointed out that the men who founded the nation and the men who led it had been men who always paused to recognize almighty God. When Patrick Henry gave his great speech that helped to give birth to this great democracy — "Give me liberty or give me death" — he also said, "There is a just God who rules over the destiny of nations." Andrew Jackson, who lived just across the Cumberland river, was the most important and influential man of his time. He was known to call on the help of almighty God. When Woodrow Wilson sent this nation across the seas, he said, "With God's help we can do no other." When Franklin Roosevelt made that memorable address on that fateful day when the Japanese attacked this nation, he closed his remarks by saying, "We shall gain the victory so help us God." I could not help but think of the thousands upon thousands who have paid the supreme sacrifice that this nation might endure, that we might have this freedom we have right here this morning.

Driving back from that cemetery I saw the Madison church building and I said to myself, "Isn't it something to live in a country where there can be a church of Christ like this, with a $3 million plant, sitting on a prominent corner with a 3,000 seat auditorium? Not only are we not afraid of the government coming here, tearing it up, shooting us, throwing us in prison, closing us up — we have it tax free. We don't pay a penny in taxes on this magnificent plant. All that we give this month can be used to preach the Gospel and to help the poor and the lowly. Can you imagine a thing like that existing today in the communist world? Do you think Hitler for a moment would have let a church of Christ of this size and potential exist in his Germany? I welcome the criticism of our nation, but I pray God it may be done within the framework of unbelievable gratitude and humility for what God has done for this country.

I appreciate what the president of the United States said when he was in Tennessee, "We welcome dissent. It is good for students to criticize; but let the Lord have mercy on that little handful of students who came to a religious service and shouted obscenities." *U.S. News and World Report* says this week that the President of the United States cannot speak on many college campuses because these people who do all of the talk about tolerance are so intolerant. Some who talk so much about wanting to be heard won't listen. I studied under some of those professors in the northern universities. They make fun of the South. They call it the Bible belt, the cesspool of fundamentalism. They chastise us for being so intolerant and can't even see how intolerant they are. It is an amazing thing how they can dish it out but can't take it. Those who cry so loud sometimes to be heard would rather cut a man's throat than listen.

I'm saying all that this morning to say this: There is a lot wrong with our country. Let us criticize it freely. Let us try to make it better. But let us never forget there is a lot right about this nation, or there wouldn't be a few thousand of us worshiping on this corner today.

And so it is with the church. There is a lot wrong. We hear it criticized on every hand. We hear its hypocrisy criticized. Let's face it: The church is made up of people. People are made of dust, and we are weak and prone to err. We have shortcomings, and there is a lot in the church that needs to be criticized. I think it is commendable that most of the criticism comes from those of us who love it. I have criticized the church from coast to coast because it does not do enough benevolent work. I have criticized its formality and coldness under the guise of dignity. As long as we are human beings, we are fallible and we need to be improved. I want our young people to criticize our lack of fervency, our lack of zeal, our lack of dedication, our lack of spirituality, our lack of depth, our lack of Bible studies, our lack of practicing what we preach. We need to be on guard. We need that criticism.

I don't suspect that there is a congregation of the church of Christ in our generation that has received criticism like this Madison Church. Many of you don't know that. But there are little, petty bulletins published by do-nothing preachers all over this country who write about the Madison Church week after week and month after month. We are not disturbed. I try not to even read them. Yet there is not a church in our generation that God has poured so many opportunities on as He has on this corner. The point I want to make today and that I want our young people to remember as long as they live is this: There is a lot right about the church. And there isn't anything wrong with the church as far as God and Christ and the Divine are concerned. That which needs to be criticized is the human side. Let us not lose our perspective.

Now I want to mention some things that are right. It has the right builder. Jesus Christ said, "Upon this rock I will build My church" (Matthew 16:18). There has never been a builder in human history who could begin to touch the hem of the garment of Jesus Christ of Nazareth. He never attended a college. He never wrote a book. He never traveled more than 100 miles from home. He died when He was 33. He was executed as a common criminal. Yet, He has inspired more millions, inspired more and better lives, inspired more Christian homes, inspired more good music, inspired more literature that elevates the human spirit than all the other men who have ever lived.

"When Jesus came into the coasts of Caesarea Philippi, he asked his disciples, saying, Whom do men say that I the Son of man am? And they said, Some say that thou art John the Baptist: some, Elias; and others, Jeremias, or one of the prophets. He saith unto them, But whom say ye that I am? And Simon Peter answered and said, Thou art the

Christ, the Son of the living God. And Jesus answered and said unto him, Blessed art thou, Simon Barjonah: for flesh and blood hath not revealed it unto thee, but my Father which is in heaven. And I say also unto thee, That thou art Peter, and upon this rock I will build my church; and the gates of hell shall not prevail against it" (Matthew 16:13-18).

There have been wars fought over the interpretation of this passage. Our Mormon friends say that the church was built on continuous revelation, and therefore God continuously reveals. This cannot be true because the Bible says that faith was once and for all delivered to the saints. Then there are friends who say the church was built on Peter, fallible fisherman Peter. This could not be true because Paul says in the Corinthian letter, "For other foundation can no man lay than that is laid, which is Jesus Christ" (1 Corinthians 3:11). The foundation of the church is Jesus the Christ. So I tell you today that the church has the right foundation and it has the right builder, and that is what is right with the Church.

The church also has the right name. "I will build my church." Paul in writing in the Roman letter says, "The churches of Christ salute you." The Church in Corinth is referred to as the church of God. The church wears the name of God and the name of Christ. The Bible says of God and Christ, "All mine are thine, and thine are mine; and I am glorified in them" (John 17:10). It is just as scriptural to say "church of God" as it is to say "church of Christ," for God and Christ and the Holy Spirit are one in purpose and one in plan. The Church wears the name that is above every name. I love the Church for the name it wears, the name of my Savior. How sweet and precious the name of Jesus is to the heart of the believer.

When the great apostle Paul was going to Jerusalem after his three missionary tours (Acts 21:10-14), the prophet Agabus told them not to go. He bound Paul's hand with his girdle, a gesture symbolic of what some Jews were going to do to Paul when he got in Jerusalem. But Paul said (paraphrasing), "Don't break my heart. Don't ask me not to go. I am going, for I am ready both to be bound and to die for the name of the Lord Jesus." I tell you a rose by any other name wouldn't smell as sweet when it comes to the name of Jesus.

The church has the right mission, the greatest mission on earth, the mission of saving sould.

Now I know there other areas when a name doesn't make any difference. We just had five little boy dogs born at our house this week. True to the North tradition, every single one of them was a male. I don't know what we are going to name those dogs. We may name one of them Lucifer and one of them Satan. I don't know. It doesn't make any difference. There are situations in life when it wouldn't make any difference, but there are also situations in life where it would make a tremendous difference. The name your wife wears makes a difference. Let her come home wearing the name of an old boy friend and let the doctors take your blood pressure then — if they have a machine that will go that high. But when it comes to the name of Jesus, it is precious, and the church wears it and that is right.

The church has the right worship. Man is a worshiping being. We must worship God in spirit and in truth, and that is what we are doing today. We are singing, and that is what the Bible says in Ephesians 5:19. We are making melody with the instrument made by God, the human heart. We have observed the Lord's Supper as taught by example, in Acts 20:7, on the first day of the week. We have read the Holy Bible, and we are studying it as the Book teaches in 2 Timothy 2:15 and other passages. Soon we shall lay by in store, as God had prospered us, on this first day of the week (1 Corinthians 16:1-2). You say, "Well these are not worship in themselves." I know they are not. Worship is an emotion of the human heart, but these are channels God has given us to express that emotion.

The church has the right organization. The Bible tells us that the church of the New Testament at the local congregation had its own elders or bishops or pastors — those who had the oversight. The church had its own deacons, evangelists, teachers, members. And that is exactly what we have here today.

I was thrilled several weeks ago when we were down at Montgomery Bell for a weekend; the elders, Brother and Sister Jones, and elders' wives. One of our elders asked Brother Jones, "Ben, you've been here a year. Why don't you give it to us straight? What do the young people think of the leadership of this church? Let us have it. We can take it."

Ben thought a minute, and he said, "Well, they are

intensely loyal to the leadership of this church."
When that meeting was over, this elder remarked,
"Do you know what the highlight of all the sessions
were? It was when Ben told us of the loyalty of the
young people to the leadership of this church." Our
young people know the Bible teaches that each congregation is to have elders to rule and to obey them
that rule over you. Rule by love, yes. Not lording it
over the flock, yes. By example, yes.

The church has the right mission, the greatest
mission on earth, the mission of saving souls. That
is what it all boils down to. It all boils down to trying to prepare men and women and boys and girls at
the age of accountability for immortality, for an eternal home. "Go ye into all the world, and preach the
Gospel to every creature" (Mark 16:15). We must be
interested in every soul, and the world includes
going across the street. In the vacation Bible school
beginning June 15 we are going to have four or five
city buses. We are going to cover this community
and then run our little buses from Hendersonville
down to a few outlying places where our members
live. Any church that will go across the ocean and
won't go across the street is bound to be ridden with
hypocrisy. It is so easy to love at long range — and
we must love at long range — but what is the matter with loving at short range? We have churches
that will get excited and do everything in the world
to go to Nigeria but won't walk across the street and
knock on a door to get a soul for Christ. The mission
of the church is right. Its mission is the salvation of
every soul that we can influence, near or far. That's
what is right about the church.

The church has the right future. There are many things that I love about the church, but this I know: When I'm associated with the church, when I'm a member of the church, I'm on a winning team. This is a marvelous thing for the people of God, but the people who do not believe can't understand it. They say, "How can you be so optimistic? How can you be so happy? How can you see the bright side when there is sin and sorrow and shame and degradation and fighting and killing and every evil form of immorality all around you?" That was the thing that shook the pagan world 2,000 years ago. In that lustful, adultery-ridden empire where there was gambling and every form of vice, here came a group of people smiling. Here came a group of people positive. Here came a group of people with an attitude they were on the winning side. The pagan world says, "What is the meaning of this?" Ladies and gentlemen, don't you worry. In the final analysis, the church is going to win. When you are with the church, you are with a winner, for you are with Christ. Someday the church shall be presented to the Father as a bride adorned for her husband without spot and without wrinkle. That is what is right with the church.

Civilizations have come and gone, but the Word of the Lord is still here. It will endure.

The last thing I want to mention is that the church has the power to endure. People say, "I just wonder if the church is going to last." Yes, it is going to last.

There is no way to destroy it. Heaven and earth shall pass away, but the seed of the kingdom, which is the Word of God (Luke 8), will never pass away. You can't destroy the Bible. They tried to burn it in the Middle Ages. Today it is the largest selling book in the world.

As long as I have a handful of hickory cane corn, I can't say that corn has perished from the earth because I can sow that corn and if the soil is prepared right it will produce. I'm having a time with my own garden this year. I have an acre and a half and every neighbor in Neely's Bend has me beat a country mile. I told an old farmer that I bought the best seed. He said, "Yes, but you plowed the ground too wet. You haven't prepared your soil right, and it is hard. You are just going to have to wait until next year and prepare it." I'll tell you, if you prepare right, it will produce. As long as I've got a handful of mustard seed, I can't say mustard has vanished from the earth. There it is.

As long as this Bible endures, you can't say the church isn't here. There it is in the seed form. When the Gospel is preached in Corinth or Rome or Thessalonica or Nashville or Ethridge or Ashland City — if it is preached like it is here and it falls on good and honest hearts it will produce the church of our Lord. Civilizations have come and gone, but the Word of the Lord is still here. It will endure.

I want our young people to know this. If you ever leave the church you leave Jesus Christ — for Christ without the church is impossible. The Word of God says that Christ is the head, and the church is the body. You can't sever the head from the body. If you do, you have life in neither. When you leave the church, you leave Jesus Christ because the Bible says in Ephesians 5 that Christ is the husband and the church is the bride. They are one. To leave the church is to leave Christ. To leave Christ is to leave all your hope. One time when they left the Lord by droves, He turned to His apostles and said, "Are you going to leave me too?" Peter said, "Lord, to whom shall we go? thou hast the words to eternal life" (John 6: 68). Peter was saying, "If we leave You, there is nowhere else to go." And that is what is right with the church. You leave it and you leave everything.

I love the kingdom because I love the church. I know it is made up of people like me. Weak, frail, made of dust and prone to err, but it is heaven born. It is blood bought. It stands for everything today that is pure and good, that is holy and right. Wherever I go on this old planet called earth, I want to be with the church. It is my life. When I've gone the last mile, don't give me a lodge, don't give me a club; give me the church. Let devout men who believe in Jesus carry my body to the silent city. Let a member of the Church read the Bible. Let another say a prayer. If there be any praise, if there be any glory, if there be any word of encouragement, let it be in the grandest, greatest, sweetest, finest, most wonderful thing this world has ever been graced with — the church of our Jesus Christ. It can be yours. Will you come today?

∽

Madison Church of Christ
Nashville, Tennessee
May 19, 1970

Look for the Providence of God

The greatest preachers I have known believed deeply, sincerely, almost passionately in the divine providence of God, our Father. I too believe in this great, fascinating, biblical principle with all my heart. I believe all who are "the called according to His purpose" — everyone who has been born of the water and the spirit, who is a member of the New Testament church — has the hand of God in his life. How bleak and barren and sad it would be if we did not really believe that "all things work together for good to them that love God, to them who are the called according to his purpose" (Romans 8:28). So let us believe fervently and passionately in the providence of God.

"Hear me when I call, O God of my righteousness: thou hast enlarged me when I was in distress" (Psalm 4:1). When sorrow or problems or mountains come, I believe God is with me and will cause that mountain to turn out to be a blessing in my life. Now, sometimes, we do not understand all of the circumstance around the providence of God, but the Bible says that we walk by faith and not by sight (2 Corinthians 5:7). We don't ask to understand everything. We ask to believe and to have faith enough to trust God, for He does all things well. If we are "the called according to His purpose," we should believe in the divine providence of God.

Let us believe fervently and passionately in the providence of God.

Let us expect the providence of God. It is not always what happens to us; it is not always the circumstance. It is our attitude toward the circumstance that is a major determining factor in the outcome of a situation. I read one time a very interesting study. A man who was an alcoholic, a bum, a poor citizen who could not hold a job, a disgrace to his family and his community, had two sons. A college ran a study on those two boys. One of them was a drunk, a bum and a disgrace. The other one was a clean, wholesome, useful citizen, a teetotaler. Both boys were asked the same question: "Why did you turn out like you did?" Both gave the same answer: "What else could you expect with a father like I had?" You see, it was not the circumstance that determined the outcome of the boys. It was rather their reaction to the circumstance. We can turn a negative happening into a blessing if we just react correctly.

"O God of my righteousness: thou hast enlarged me when I was in distress." It is a way of saying, "Thank you, Lord, for the possibilities pregnant in every problem." There are possibilities for good in every difficulty if only we learn to look for and to expect to see the hand of God. Let's expect some good from every happening in our lives, for we love God and are "the called according to His purpose."

One of my favorite texts to illustrate this is Acts 8. A great persecution came against the church of Christ in Jerusalem nearly 2,000 years ago. The persecutions ran the Christians out of town and took their homes away from them. I'm sure there might have been some negative brothers, even then, who would wring their hands and say, "Well, this is the end of Christianity; it certainly is the end of the church. This great church of 5,000 men, not counting women and children, has had everything taken away from them." But it was not the end of Christianity; it was just the beginning. The Bible says, "They went every where preaching the word." And soon there were great churches all over the civilized world. Some Bible scholars think the church in Antioch was far larger than the church in Jerusalem. My guess is that the church in Ephesus was larger than the one in Jerusalem. From what some thought was a tragedy, there came great spiritual blessings.

Let us learn to look for the providence of God, for the beautiful act of God in our life. Many times we do not see the providence of God because we are not looking for it. It is amazing, sometimes, how we find what we are looking for. We live on a farm on the river here in Madison. I love the farm. I hope I don't love it too much. It is so peaceful and quiet. Occasionally, I see an old buzzard flying over the farm, and it flies and flies. Do you know what he is looking for? He is looking for something nasty and something dead. He just keeps sailing around until he finds it. Sometimes I see a hummingbird flying around that same farm, and he will find thousands of beautiful flowers and vines to enjoy. Now all those beautiful things were there for the vulture, but the vulture was not looking for the beautiful and the good and the true and the lovely. It is amazing how so often in life we find what we are looking for. We do not look for the divine providence of God our Father.

We are sometimes by nature prone to look for the negative. You know the bad things always make the headlines. That used to disturb me greatly. I think I understand it now, partly because the bad is really the exception. If all the good things that happened to the people of God in Nashville this last week were published in today's edition of the Sunday paper, it would be two feet thick. In fact those multi-million dollar presses down there on Broadway couldn't publish this week the wonderful, beautiful things that have happened to the 5,000 people who call the Madison Church home. Oh yes, we are all sinners (Romans 3:23), and I think that most of us are, by nature, geared for the negative. We expect the negative — unless Christ Jesus has touched our lives.

If Christ and His love dominate our thinking and our lives, then the negative emotions of anger, jealousy, envy, distrust, suspicion, scorn and bitterness are replaced by the positive emotions of love, forgiveness, trust and peace. When we are not in touch with God, when we are out of touch with Christ, we look for the bad. We expect the bad. We become cynical, bitter and hostile instead of loving, forgiving, kind, hopeful and joyful. A person out of touch with God hungers for the negative; the person out of touch with God hungers for suspicion, anger, distrust and hostility. He hungers to hear failure stories. But I believe in the providence of God. I look for the providence of God, and I expect the providence of God.

It is amazing how so often in life we find what we are looking for.

Sometimes we say, "All right, we are to believe in the providence of God. We ought to expect it and we ought to look for it. But where and how can we find it?" I want to give a suggestion today that I believe will be practical and helpful. If you want to see the providence of God in your life, look for problems, look for a mountain. Many times God reaches us in a moment of pain. I think, sometimes, there is no gain without pain. Maybe that is why the Lord said, "Blessed are they that mourn: for they shall be comforted" (Matthew 5:4).

Before a man succeeds in almost any field that I know anything about there is some pain. You can take any field. Take law. A man who is a good lawyer, has to finish high school, four years of college, and three years of law school. It is not over then. He has to take the bar exam, which is one of the few times in his life when he feels like everything depends on one examination. Then after he passes, if he doesn't work like a dog, he will just be a "jack-leg" lawyer. It takes a lot of hard work and pain to produce a man skilled in the law to help people.

Take the field of medicine. I don't know of a doctor serving humanity today who hasn't suffered a few years of pain. He goes 12 years to finish high school, four years in college, three years in medical school, one year as an intern, two years as a resident, and maybe two to four years in the Army. Then at the age of 33 — when his wife has spent everything she can rake and scrape; his mom and dad are flat broke; his grandparents are tired of paying the bills — then he can go into private practice and make a living. He and his family have experienced a lot of pain, but where there is no pain, there is no gain.

What is true in the law and medicine is true in the ministry and every field. When the mountains come and when problems come, they never leave us where they find us. I don't think trouble has ever left a man where it found him. It either leaves him bitter and cold; harsh and cynical; distrusting and angry; or it leaves him more compassionate, sympathetic, loving, forgiving and understanding. I always make this point when I preach the funeral of a child who has died. I say, "This tragedy will not leave you the same. From this day forward, you will be different people. You will either be more compassionate, sympathetic, understanding, loving, helpful and considerate of others in sorrow, you will be bitter, cold and cynical."

Do you remember a song a few years ago by one of these Nashville crooners: "Lord, you have given me a mountain"? By the end of the song, his wife (or girlfriend) has left him and he sings, "Lord, this time, you have really given me a mountain."

Well, why does God give us mountains? Everybody in here either has had some mountains or will have before you die. Why does God give us mountains? I want to mention a few reasons in order to help you spot the providence of God, to look for the providence of God, to expect the providence of God, to see the providence of God, and to trust the providence of God.

Sometimes God gives a mountain to block us, to keep us from running too far ahead and getting into trouble, and to keep us from getting into enemy territory. I am quite sure that I have flown over a million miles in my ministry, including across the ocean seven times, but only one time have I missed a speaking engagement because of plane trouble. Once I was in Memphis on my way to speak in Dallas at 7 o'clock. It was 5:30, and the pilot said, "Ladies and gentlemen, we are going to leave this plane in Memphis. One of these engines doesn't sound right to me. You will get off this plane, and another one will pick you up an hour or two later." Some of the passengers complained about it, but I didn't. I believed the providence of God brought that about. I missed that engagement in Dallas, but I have made hundreds and hundreds and hundreds since then that I wouldn't have made if that plane had taken off and not made it. Sometimes God puts a mountain in our life to stop us, to block us, to keep us out of enemy territory. "In my distress thou hast enlarged me."

Sometimes He gives us a mountain to mature us, to give us time to grow up spiritually, to enable us to stand when the great opportunities come. When Moses was 40 years old, he thought he was ready. He had the finest education the world could offer, everything money could buy, plus great faith in God. He thought he was ready, but God put a mountain and blocked him. God took him away to the desert and let him spend 40 years. Why? God had in mind for that man to lead the greatest human exodus known in history. Moses was not quite ready; he needed to mature more; he needed a few more years to think, to study, to pray and to learn. God sent him a mountain.

Sometimes God gives us a mountain to humble us.

When I was teaching at David Lipscomb College, I saw this several times. A young man from another state came to Lipscomb. He was 17 years old, a freshman in college, and had a marvelous gift of speech. He was very articulate, very sharp, and he had possibilities of being a great preacher. He came to my office one day and said, "Brother North, I want a place to preach." I said, "Well, the Bear Wallow Church just called me, and they want me to find a preacher. I think it would be wonderful for you, and they are going to pay $5. It will cost you only about $3 to get there and back; that will leave you $2." He said, "I am insulted. I'll have you know that I have been preaching five years. So-n-So is preaching at a congregation here in town, and he has just two years' experience. They are paying him $30 a week." I said, "My friend, you do not understand. You are 17; you are not dry behind the ears; you are green. You ought to pay them to hear you. This young man that you are talking about is 25 years old and has done a hitch in the United States Army. He is mature; you are green."

Well, I want to tell you the outcome of that boy. Before he got out of his teens, he was a veteran preacher of seven years, had quit preaching, and had quit the church before his 20th birthday. I think the people who started him preaching down in Alabama were honest, good, conscientious and sincere, but they sinned grievously against the boy. He thought preaching was glamorous and marvelous. When he got into it and saw what guts and determination and prayer and defeat a preacher goes through, it floored him and he couldn't take it. Sometimes God gives us a mountain to mature us. He wants us, when the disappointments come, to be strong enough to stand.

Sometimes God gives us a mountain to humble us, to remind us that "it is not in man that walketh to direct his steps" (Jeremiah 10:23). This was the very case in 2 Corinthians 12 with the apostle Paul. God gave him a mountain in the form of an aggravating, thorn in the flesh. We don't know what the thorn was. Some think he was near-sighted: He couldn't see well and was traveling around preaching the Gospel nearly blind. Others think he was crippled; others think he had some form of disease. At any rate, the problem was humiliating to Paul. He said that he had prayed three times and asked God to take this thorn away. I think we can paraphrase and say, "Take this mountain away, Lord." God said to Paul each time, "My grace is sufficient." Paul explains that through his weakness, the strength of God was made known. Paul explains that it has kept me reminded that the power is not in me but in the message that I preach and in the Christ that I proclaim. Sometimes God gives us a mountain to humble us.

God sometimes gives a mountain to strengthen us, to build our spiritual muscles, to make us mete for the Master's use, to let us grow up to the fullness of the stature of Christ Jesus, our Lord.

Bow with me and let us pray: O God, our Father, teach us to believe in Your divine providence, for we are Your children. O God, our Father, teach us to expect in our lives the beautiful acts of Your divine providence. Teach us to look for Your divine providence. Oh God, free us from the negative that would create in us the bitter, cynical, heartless and cold. Instead, let us, through Christ, be filled with love and trust and joy and peace. Oh God, thank You for the mountains You have given us: mountains to stop us, mountains to mature us, mountains to humble us, mountains to strengthen us. Oh God, thank You for the mountains You have given the Madison Church of Christ. We thank You for that mountain of debt in paying for this auditorium, for it has helped us to be liberal and taught us to depend on You. Thank You for the mountains and problems that we face in our child care program. It has taught us to love the humble and lowly. Thank You for the mountains You have given us in this television and radio ministry. We thank You for all of them. Now if there is one here who has never named the sweet name of Jesus, never been baptized into Christ for the remission of sins, we pray that he will do so now that he may be with us — through Your grace — "the called according to Your purpose." For we pray in the name of Jesus the Christ, Amen.

∽

Madison Church of Christ
Madison, Tennessee
August 31, 1975

All Things Work Together for Good

For our Bible lesson today, I'm sharing with you one of the great texts of the Bible. I think when properly understood, it is one of the most comforting and powerful passages in all of Holy Writ. Life will be richer, and deeper, and sweeter, and finer if we understand and accept this passage.

"And we know that all things work together for good to them that love God, to them who are the called according to his purpose" (Romans 8:28).

Now there are those who say that all things work together for good in every circumstance. That isn't true. The text does say "all things work together for good." Then it gives qualifications and conditions that we must believe and accept. There are some who think that whatever happens is bound for good. Well, the man with that attitude is not believing a doctrine of faith. He is believing a doctrine of fate. That doctrine is false to the core. We want to believe and trust not a doctrine of fate that everything works out for good but a doctrine of faith that "all things work together for good to them that love the Lord and are the called according to his purpose."

The Bible doesn't say that everything that happens will be good.

There are several things I want you to note with me about the text. Then I want us to consider three Bible illustrations and three Bible examples of the truthfulness of this great biblical principle.

First of all, please note that the text does not say that everything that happens will be good. I couldn't tell a young couple that it was a good thing that their three-month-old son had a terminal blood disease. That was tragic and heart breaking. It was sad to the extreme. But I did tell them that even in a tragedy like this, if they would love the Lord and be true to His purposes, the Almighty would work it out some way for their good. No, the Bible doesn't say that everything that happens will be good.

Some tragic, terrible things happen to good and wonderful people. The Bible tells us how one of the best men who ever lived, Job, lost every material thing, and he was a man of fortune with a lot to lose. The Bible tells that he was a good man who lost his health, but in it all he said something akin to, "I don't understand it, but I trust God." "Naked came I out of my mother's womb, and naked shall I return thither: the Lord gave, and the Lord hath taken away; blessed be the name of the Lord. In all this Job sinned not, nor charged God foolishly" (Job 1:21-22).

The second thing I want you to note with me about the text is that God does not promise His divine providence for foolish action. The doctrine that everything is going to work out is fate and not faith. If I act foolishly, I don't need to think that everything is going to work out for good.

For example, I have a son who went to school out in Texas and he was in the "fast-draw club." I said, "Well, man, that is dangerous." He said, "Oh, they just shoot blanks." He called me one day and said, "Dad, I shot myself today." And I said, "No, you couldn't shoot yourself because you just use blanks." He said, "Dad, I have a confession to make." I said, "What confession do you have to make?" He said, "It wasn't a blank. I have a bullet in the calf of my leg." I said, "What does the doctor say?" He said, "It will do more harm to take it out, so we'll leave it in. I'll have to carry it all my life." I said, "Well that is a pretty good Texas souvenir. Next time tell your daddy the truth." I still wonder how he got the money to get that Texas revolver. You could take one of those Texas revolvers with six chambers and one bullet in it — they call that Russian Roulette — and put it to your head and say, "All things work out." Well, I'll tell you one thing, you got one chance in six. I can also tell you how it is eventually going to work out: You are going to scatter your brains and face God unprepared. I hate to say it like it really is, but you have one chance in six of blowing your brains out and going to hell forever. That is what can happen.

We need to know this passage does not, never has, and never will include foolish actions. You can't sit on a railroad track and say, "Everything is going to work out." If a train is coming at 90 miles an hour and you sit on the track, I'll tell you how it is going to work out: You are going to be smashed to smithereens. You acted foolishly; you didn't use the good judgment that God gave you. If you love the Lord and are tuned in to His purposes, you won't be sitting out there on the railroad track with a train coming 90 miles an hour. We need to understand this principle and not use this great text as a cover up to teach something it doesn't teach.

Every child ought to be taught two things: to do with and to do without.

About 20 years ago when I was down in the little cubbyhole office in the basement at the Madison Church, a young man came to see me. He was in financial difficulty, and I talked with him awhile. I took a pencil, and I said, "Let's see how much you owe." "Well, I got a certain amount on this and on this and that." We added it up, and I said, "You have $400 going out and $300 coming in. I don't have a Ph.D. in mathematics, but you don't have to have a third-grade education to know what is going to happen. When your 'out-go' is more than your 'in-come' it is your 'undo.' I'll tell you what kind of foolish action that is going to do to you: You are going to go bankrupt. You are going to lose your reputation. You are going to have a reputation as a crook, not an honest man. You don't pay your debts, and you are going to walk in a bank someday and need $10,000. Instead of that banker putting his hand on your shoulder and saying, 'Son, I've known you for years; you're an honest man. Sign your name and get whatever you want,' he is going to say, 'Look, I wouldn't loan you $10.' "

I got specific with him, "What about this big, shining gas-guzzler you have out here? The payment was $125." I did the worst thing I could have done to a young fellow. I said, "Look, son, a man making $300 a month can't afford that big, shiny gas-guzzler with a payment of $125 a month." That really shook him up, and he said, "Brother North, what did you do when you were my age?" I said, "I remember it, and what I did I despised and hated. I rode the Nashville transit system in town, and out of town I rode the Greyhound bus. When I went to preach at Midway in Lawrence County, I rode in on the Greyhound bus. Then the people from the church took me to the bus station and I rode out. I didn't like it, and I wanted what you have worse than anything in the world. Any young man wants wheels — shiny wheels — gas-guzzling wheels, big wheels, big payments. It makes you feel like a big man. When we rolled through Mount Pleasant on that un-air-conditioned Greyhound bus, I wiped the perspiration off my brow (it was more like Mount Misery than Mount Pleasant), and I said to myself, 'Someday I'm going to roll through here with my own automobile; I'm going to go into Lawrenceburg in style.' But I didn't have the money to ride in my own automobile, so I rode the bus."

I don't mean to blame this on the young people, though you need it. Every child ought to be taught two things: to do with and to do without. Your old dad taught you to do with, but where your dad slipped up in our affluent age was he didn't teach you to do without. You've never done without anything in your life. So it is a bitter pill to act responsible when you become 21 years of age.

God does not promise His divine providence for foolish action. ... If I act foolishly, I don't need to think that everything is going to work out for good.

The principle I want to drive home for all of us is this passage does not cover foolish acts. It just doesn't do it. Those of us who are older need this lesson; I need it. We are building a log cabin down on the river. Abraham Lincoln was born in a log cabin. I wonder if log cabins were as expensive back then as they are now. We have it half done, and the money is two-thirds gone. I sent word to the contractor to leave off the screened porch, the fence, the storage, and the hitching rail. We may be on orange crates as you come in and you say, "Oh, is this the latest from Chicago?" I'll say, "No this is the latest thing from Compton's Bi-Rite." We have to be careful, and those of us who are older must set the right example in acting responsible.

The saddest illustration that I know of took place in Oklahoma. A few years ago some young people were having fun, and came to an old strip in the road and they started playing chicken. One car would come head-on at another car, and the first car that swerved was chicken. That is not bravery; that is not courage; that is not responsibility. That is foolishness. We might have said, "Oh, well, whatever happens will be for the best." I could have told them what was likely to happen. It did happen. Someone called the hospital and asked, "What about So-n-So? How is she doing?" They said, "She is not here; she is at the funeral home. She passed away, killed in that accident."

If we love the Lord, are in tune with His purposes, and are a part of the called out which is the church of our Lord (the kingdom of God), then all things work together for good. Whatever happens — good or bad, little or big, here or there — it will all be worked out by the loving, heavenly Father for our good. We just want to be sure that we love the Lord and that we are, to the best of our ability, doing right and are attuned to His purposes.

There are three illustrations that I call your attention to. All are very familiar. I think the most familiar passage in all the Old Testament is the one about the man who has been called the best moral man in the Old Testament. I don't know if that is true or not, but I do know this: The Bible tells it like it is. As far as I know, there is not one derogatory word said about this good man. Preachers through the years have used the story of his life as an example of the powerful providence of almighty God in the lives of His children when we love Him, trust Him, and stay in tune with His purposes. It is the case of Joseph, a young man sold as a slave at 17 and thrown in prison by a conniving and wicked woman. After he was in prison, he was betrayed by his friends. Finally through the providence of almighty God, who protected him and cared for him, Joseph was put in a place of responsibility and great honor. He saved not only Egypt but all the civilized world from starvation, including the little land of Israel from which would come the nation of Israel and Christ Jesus, our Lord.

Do you remember when Joseph's brothers finally came? I want you to imagine with me how you would feel if you had helped to sell your brother as a slave. Now he is prime minister and has the power of life and death over you and he reveals himself to you. Here you are standing before him, knowing you had treated him like that. How would you feel?

The Bible says in Genesis 45:4-11, "And Joseph said unto his brethren, Come near to me, I pray you. And they came near. And he said, I am Joseph your brother, whom ye sold into Egypt. Now therefore be not grieved, nor angry with yourselves, that ye sold me hither: for God did send me before you to preserve life. For these two years hath the famine been in the land: and yet there are five years, in the which there shall neither be earing nor harvest. And God sent me before you to preserve you a posterity in the earth, and to save your lives by a great deliverance. So now it was not you that sent me hither, but God: and he hath made me a father to Pharaoh, and lord of all his house, and a ruler throughout all the land of Egypt. Haste ye, and go up to my father, and say unto him, Thus saith thy son Joseph, God hath made me lord of all Egypt: come down unto me, tarry not: And thou shalt dwell in the land of Goshen, and thou shalt be near unto me, thou, and thy children, and thy children's children, and thy flocks, and thy herds, and all that thou hast: And there will I nourish thee; for yet there are five years of famine; lest thou, and thy household, and all that thou hast, come to poverty."

Joseph says, "You meant it for evil, but God worked it out for good." But remember — Joseph loved the Lord. What if Joseph had not loved the Lord? What if he had not been in tune with the purposes of God? It would have been a different story.

We just want to be sure that we love the Lord and that we are, to the best of our ability, doing right and are attuned to His purposes.

I call your attention next to a New Testament illustration that I think points clearly to what we are talking about. Look at Acts 16. You remember that Paul saw the vision of Macedonia? "Come over and help us." He and his companions went to Philippi, the largest city in Macedonia. An unfortunate and mentally ill girl followed them crying out, "These men are the servants of the most high God" (Acts 16:17). What she said was right, but it was irritating and embarrassing to have such ignoble means of declaring such a high and holy truth. I can understand that. I've never known how to handle a case of mental illness when it shows in the church.

For example, I remember when I was 18 years old, and I was preaching in a meeting at Midway. A man came forward and wanted to be baptized. Well, I had been warned that this brother was off mentally, that he came forward every time, and that he had been baptized a half-dozen times. When I was told that, I said, "Well, I'm not going to baptize him again." When he came forward and told me that he wanted to be baptized, I said, "Brother, you have been baptized over and over again. I want to talk to you after the service." Then I told the audience, "Ladies and gentlemen, I want to talk to this brother after the service. I believe he needs some private teaching." I talked to him afterwards. The next night he did the same thing, and I did the same thing. Each time I told him, "You've been baptized like the Bible says; you are a member of the church. If you have sinned publicly, you need to come back, but you don't need to come forward every time we have a service." Well, he did. I was embarrassed by it, but I believe the people understood. I can understand a little bit of how Paul felt.

Paul turned around and ordered the demon in this woman to come out. I don't know exactly what Paul did. We don't know much now about mental illness. I know that depression, when it sinks below a certain point and stays there, is a real demon. It leads to insanity, and suicide and a lot of other negative actions. We all have our ups and downs. That is all right. But it is when you get down there and stay, that you are in deep trouble. None of us understands all about mental illness. But this girl was sick, and Paul made her well.

When she was made well those evil men in Philippi who were using her unfortunate condition for financial gain were mad about it, and they intended to get the preacher. What they did was to trump up a charge. They said, "Well, he is preaching

tradition; he is not loyal to Rome." They had Paul
and Silas, another marvelous preacher, thrown into
prison. They were beaten, and their hands and feet
were put in stocks where they couldn't sit up and
they couldn't lean back and be comfortable.

You know what happened at midnight? They were
singing and praying and suddenly the doors opened
in an earthquake. The jailer knew he would have to
give his own life for the life of the people who escaped.
No doubt to save his family from shame and disgrace,
he sought to take his own life. But Paul said, "Do thyself no harm: for we are all here." And he fell down
and said, "Sirs, what must I do to be saved?" He knew
these men had to be from God. "Believe on the Lord
Jesus and thou shalt be saved, and thy house." Then
Paul preached to the jailer and his family about
Christ, and the same hour of the night he took them
and baptized them (Acts 16:19-33).

Don't you know that Paul and Silas could talk
later about how wonderful it was that God worked
out that terrible experience when they were put in
jail and beaten unjustly. From that experience came
the conversion of the jailer. Later on one of the great
churches of the first century grew in Philippi.

The Lord worked it together for good. Paul
believed that God worked for good throughout his
imprisonments and hardships. He says in the
Roman letter and in the Philippian letter that God's
hand was present even in prison: "But I would ye
should understand, brethren, that the things which
happen unto me have fallen out rather unto the fur-
therance of the gospel" (Philippians 1:12). I've been
in jail; that is true. Note verse 13: "So that my bonds

in Christ are manifest in all the palace, and all other places." Paul is saying, "Even being in jail, God has worked out things for good. I've been able to convert others, to teach others, and others seeing me in chains are willing to stand for the truth too."

Yes, these stories illustrate the great principle that all things work together for good if we love the Lord and if we are the called according to His purpose. Will you decide today to love God? If you are here today and you have never obeyed the Gospel of Christ, I invite you to come, believing in Christ, turning from your sins, confessing His name and being baptized for remission of your sins.

∾

Madison Church of Christ
Nashville, Tennessee
July 30, 1980, a.m.

Integrity:
The Most Needed
Word

The Bible is always up to date and always new. I believe the Holy Bible gives us instructions on a subject that is so needed today. I suggest that the most needed word in the English language for this particular time in history is integrity. The Bible is up to date on integrity. We need integrity so desperately today. We define integrity as "the finest in moral principle, character, uprightness, and honesty."

We need integrity in government. I plead with our young people not to become cynical or bitter and not to think that all of our public officials accept bribes and are dishonest. We have had some things happen in this country recently that have really shaken us up. Some of the highest officials in the land have accepted thousands of dollars in a brown envelope and have been disbarred. But it is still true that an honest citizen can run for a high office in the government and can be elected. We have seen it in

Nashville. I understand that 2,500 hours were spent by the opposition of a man who has just been elected to run for the U.S. Senate trying to find a flaw in the candidate's character. Can you imagine? Twenty-five hundred hours by experts looking into the background of this boy from the fields. They were trying to find a breach in his character, trying to find a breach in his integrity. But he lived such a clean life, loyal to his church, reared by a father and mother who believed in integrity. Nothing was found, not even after searching 2,500 hours by experts. The time may well come in America, and I pray that our young people will help bring it about, that not only can a man with integrity be elected, but that *only* a man with integrity can be elected to public trust and public service. If Christian people would work at it and young people would back that philosophy, it could come about.

We need integrity in business. I admire the small business men and women of America who have succeeded through honesty, hard work, diligent toil and integrity. I was by the Stop and Shop grocery where I saw Sarah Compton at the cash register. J. R. was in the back working at the meat counter at their family business. I saw that in my father and mother's undertaking business. My father did the embalming and conducted the funerals, and my mother kept the books and ran the office. When I see small business people making a business go through hard work, honesty, uprightness and integrity, it thrills me. That is wonderful.

In big business we need to return to integrity. Terrible things have happened in this country in the last few years in big business. We are legally giving thousands and thousands of dollars to influence governmental policy. We need young men who will say, "If this business can pay a fair return and be run with integrity, we will pay a fair return. If it can't, we will pay no return." Integrity must be maintained.

How we need integrity among the professionals today. We need doctors who will not lie or overcharge, who won't take advantage of government or the rich or the poor, and who will do what is right because it is right. We need lawyers who have integrity. Teachers, educators, union leaders, and people in every phase of our national and our economic life in America — what we need is people of integrity.

The greatest legacy a man can give his son or daughter is integrity. It is a hundred times better to leave children a legacy of integrity than to leave them silver and gold.

The Bible has a lot to say about integrity, and I want to share some of it with you today. In the Old Testament the law required integrity. Deuteronomy 16:18-20 deals great trust in any man who takes public office in the judiciary. The Bible says, "Thou shalt not wrest judgment; thou shalt not respect persons, neither take a gift."

A man who is poor ought to have his rights protected with equal vigor as a man who is rich. In the church we need to learn this. James 2:9 says, "But if ye have respect to persons, ye commit sin." A man comes in with a gold ring, nice clothes. You set him on the front seat and you bow and paw and scrape and cater to him. A man comes in in poor clothes, and you set him down in the back and pay no attention to him. James says, "Ye do sin. You are showing respect of persons."

Going back to Deuteronomy the text continues, "Neither take a gift: for a gift doth blind the eyes of the wise, and pervert the words of the righteous." I admire men in public office who will not accept any gift of any value. Some set a $5 value limit, and any gift that is given worth more than $5 is given to charity. They say, "I am in a position of power, and I cannot afford to be in a position that would pervert or corrupt the sacred trust."

Then the text goes on and says, "That which is altogether just shalt thou follow, that thou mayest live, and inherit the land which the Lord thy God giveth thee." So in the Old Testament integrity was required under the law: no respecter of persons; be that which is absolutely just; take no gifts, no bribes.

Then the Bible describes integrity in Proverbs. "The integrity of the upright shall guide them: but the perverseness of transgressors shall destroy them. ... the righteousness of the perfect shall direct his way" (Proverbs 11:3, 5). Then the wise man says, "The just man walketh in his integrity: his children are blessed after him" (Proverbs 20:7). I love that passage, don't you? The greatest legacy a man can give his son or daughter is integrity. It is a hundred times better to leave children a legacy of integrity than to leave them silver and gold, which can corrupt and damn them — or power, which could devour them.

How many of us in this auditorium have been blessed not because of anything we have done, but because of the integrity of some good mother or grandmother, or the integrity of some father or grandfather? David instructed his people to deal kindly with a boy, Mephibosheth, for his father's (Jonathan's) sake (2 Samuel 9). He was saying, "If you find him, be good to him for his old dad's sake."

Then the Bible teaches us that in resisting temptation we must have integrity. There is no substitute for it. In Genesis 39:8-9 we have one of the most powerful stories in all the Bible of how integrity is the greatest thing against temptation. You remember Joseph was sold as a slave at 17. But he was an unusual lad. There is not a doubt in my mind but that he was handsome and had charisma. The boy had everything: looks, brains, character. Even when Joseph was a slave, Potiphar saw the tremendous value in that man. So Joseph became Potiphar's business manager. The truth of it is that Potiphar didn't know his own business. He turned it all over to Joseph, and he didn't withhold anything from him.

Then the Bible tells us about Potiphar's wife. No doubt she found Joseph, because he was clean and good and handsome, a temptation to her pride. She must have thought, "If I can mislead this fellow, I'm really something." Listen to what the Bible says, "But he refused, and said unto his master's wife, Behold, my master wotteth not what is with me in the house, and he hath committed all that he hath to my hand; There is none greater in this house than I; neither hath he kept back anything from me but thee, because thou art his wife: How then can I do this great wickedness and sin against God?"

What kept Joseph from sinning? He had every reason to sin, from the human standpoint. This woman was powerful; she could take his life; she could throw him in prison. It was not a little set of rules outside that kept him from sinning: it was something from within. This man had been taught by his daddy that Jehovah was God. He had learned that regardless of where you are, you do right because it is right to do right; you believe and serve the Almighty God. Joseph's actions were not based on something without but within.

You do right when everybody around you does wrong, not because of a little set of rules ... but because from within your own heart you love the Lord and trust God.

I know some of you may be thinking: "Look what happened. He was thrown in prison." That is right. Maybe it is great to go to prison when you go there for a just and right cause. Some of the greatest men who ever lived went to prison, including the apostle Paul, who probably was executed from a Roman jail. I tell you right now: You need integrity — holding to that belief in God, that wanting to be wholesome and upright because of our faith.

Our Brother Ben Jones is to be commended on this point. He taught for 10 years at the student center at the University of Arizona. Brother Ben has tried to teach our young people to do right not because of a little set of rules or because somebody is standing over you with a club or somebody is going to get after you if you don't — but you do right when you are winning and you do right when you are losing. You do right when everybody around you does wrong, not because of a little set of rules and somebody is really going to slap you if you don't, but because from within your own heart you love the Lord and trust God. Jesus Christ reigns in your heart. Because of the intensity of your heart and soul, you do right.

The Bible gives us an illustration not only of integrity and resisting temptation, but of integrity and honest administration, in the case of Samuel. You remember in 1 Samuel 12 the Israelites wanted a king. So Samuel called them all together, and they said, "Thou hast not defrauded us, nor oppressed us, neither hast thou taken ought of any man's hand. And he said unto them, The Lord is witness against you, and his anointed is witness this day, that ye have not found ought in my hand. And they answered, He is witness" (1 Samuel 12:4-5).

Samuel was saying, "Now you are asking for a king. I want you to know this, I have been ruling over you because it was the will of God that you have a judge. I haven't taken anything that doesn't belong to me. I'm calling you for witness. You have had an honest administration." They said, "Yes, we witness and we agree."

Job is another great example of integrity — the completeness of character, honesty and uprightness. You know Job lost his fortune, and that is enough to make many a man bitter. He had a good family, and he lost all of his children; that is enough to make a man bitter. I have seen some people lose one child and turn against God and become bitter. Job lost not only his wealth and his children, but he lost his health; that is enough to make a man bitter. Then he lost his friends. Last — after losing his wealth, his children, his friends, his health — he lost the moral support of his wife. She said, "Curse God and die" (Job 2:9). I want you to listen to what Job said: "My lips shall not speak wickedness, nor my tongue utter deceit. God forbid that I should justify you: till I die I will not remove mine integrity from me" (Job 27;4,5). All I have left is my integrity but I will not leave it. "Naked came I out of my mother's womb, and naked shall I return thither: the Lord gave, and the Lord hath taken away; blessed be the name of the Lord" (Job 1:21). No wonder the Bible says, "Hast thou considered my servant Job, that there is none like him in the earth?" (Job 1:8) Integrity is so important.

The Bible teaches in the Old Testament, and I believe there is a great lesson for members of the church of Christ in this, that compared to religious rights, integrity is far more important. I want you to listen to this: "Will the Lord be pleased with thousands of rams, or with ten thousands of rivers of oil? ... He hath shewed thee, O man, what is good; and what doth the Lord require of thee, but to do justly, and to love mercy, and to walk humbly with thy God" (Micah 6:7,8). Again in 1 Samuel, "Hath the Lord as great delight in burnt offerings and sacrifices, as in obeying the voice of the Lord? Behold, to obey is better than sacrifice, and to hearken than the fat of rams" (15:22). It is important to take the Lord's Supper; it is important to meet to worship; I'm not denying that. It is important to sing, and it is important to pray. But all that cannot be a cover-up for integrity. All that cannot take the place of upright living, honesty and character. Integrity is essential. Integrity shall have its reward.

I have great confidence in our young people in this church, and I believe this church is in great hands in the days ahead. I believe there will be a Madison Church of Christ as long as there is a United States of America because I believe we have young people in this church who are men and young women of integrity. Friday night we had a group down to our house on the farm just for a visit. Some of our senior boys and girls had said, "Brother North, we don't get to see you much. You don't wade the creek with us like you used to with the kids. We want to get to know you." So we had a group down, and it rained. We had the wiener roast in the basement, and we decided to go ahead on the hay ride even in the rain. Then we came in to the fireplace and dried off for a devotional.

I wish you could have heard those young men pray. I tell you, the junior and senior men in this church are young men of integrity. When they pray, they just open up their hearts and talk to God.

Most of us have been taught a few phrases: "Guide, guard and direct us" and "if we have been faithful unto Thee." That is all right. We do the best we can. That is what we have been taught. But I tell you, when these young men pray, they don't say a few memorized phrases that have been passed from generation to generation. They open their hearts and talk to God. It is a fine thing to hear them pray.

I trust the young men and women of this church. I would trust them around the world, and I believe they would have done right in Egypt. I believe they will do right in Alabama and in the University of Tennessee. I believe they will do right in the years ahead because of the word we are talking about today, which is taught in the Holy Scriptures and is so needed: *integrity*.

The Bible teaches us integrity will be rewarded. Hear Proverbs 28:20: "A faithful man shall abound with blessings." And listen now to Psalm 18:20: "The Lord rewarded me according to my righteousness; according to the cleanness of my hands he recompensed me."

I believe the great need of our day, of our age and time, is integrity. I believe through the Lord Jesus Christ and the teachings of the Holy Bible we are to be loyal to integrity of heart and integrity of soul. We believe in sound moral principle and purity and uprightness and honesty because we love the Lord and because we believe in His Word. May God forgive us when we have erred. From this day forward may we try to live like Job and Joseph and Samuel and the heroes of the Bible who were men of integrity. Will you come?

∽

Madison Church of Christ
Madison, Tennessee
June 2, 1974, a.m.

Companions in Crime: Evil Tongue and Evil Ear

Our lesson text is James 1:26: "If any man among you seem to be religious, and bridleth not his tongue, but deceiveth his own heart, this man's religion is vain."

This lesson is a review of an article by Frank Cox on the same subject: "An Evil Tongue and an Evil Ear." Really an evil tongue wouldn't be much harm unless there was an evil ear to listen to that evil tongue. They are indeed companions in crime.

It is a very serious thing to commit a crime, and it is a very serious thing to be a companion in crime. I can remember an incident during my youth in Middle Tennessee and I want to share it with you for the benefit of all our boys and girls here today. You know, when you are young you can cross the line from a prank into a crime before you know it. That is why we caution our boys and girls to try to associate with those who want to do right, who love the Lord, and who make an honest effort because no one is safe in the wrong crowd. None of us are. You remember that Peter cursed and swore when he got with the wrong crowd. He swore that he never knew the Lord. You know, Lot wasn't safe in the wrong crowd. You and I are not safe in the wrong crowd either.

Really an evil tongue wouldn't be much harm unless there was an evil ear to listen to that evil tongue. They are indeed companions inc rime.

I can remember this incident so vividly. On Halloween a couple of boys in our small town decided to have a little fun. There isn't anything wrong in having a little fun as long as it is within the framework of what is legal. We had an old brother in this little town who had an automobile. The two boys said, "We are going to go for a ride in Mr. So-n-So's automobile."

So they got in his car and they rode around the square. We just had one square in Ethridge. They met three boys and said, "Man, are we having fun! Come and go riding with us." Two of them said, "We live three miles out in the country. Would you take us home?" They said, "Sure, we are just having fun. Get in." One of the boys said, "Not on your life. I'll walk the three miles." They said, "You are stupid. Why walk three miles when you can ride in the rumble seat of this up-to-date car?" I'll never forget the one boy, whose nickname was Puney, said, "You heard me right. I'm going to walk."

The two got in, and the four drove out in the country three miles. The two boys had stolen the car let those two out and came back. They were on the way to take the car back and didn't really intend to steal it. They said, "We will just borrow it a few minutes and have a little more fun." But just before they got to the old brother's house, they rounded the curve and wrecked the car. When they wrecked the car, they became frightened and ran.

Well, in Ethridge, it wasn't hard to find out who was guilty. There is one thing about a small town where everybody knows everybody else and everybody knows everybody else's business — you don't get away with nothing. It wasn't 12 o'clock the next day until they caught all four of the boys. When they brought them up in front of the judge — he was a wise old man who knew the Scriptures — the two boys who took a ride home said, "Judge, all we did was ride in the car." The judge said, "Haven't you ever heard: 'He that biddeth him God speed is partaker of his evil deed'? All four of you are in on this, and here is what I'm going to do. I'm going to fine each one of you. You are going to fix the car up and pay the fine. I'm going to put you on probation."

One of the boys, whose name was Shorty, just didn't have any money. But he did get a job from Mr. Sam Lentz chopping wood at 10 cents an hour. After school for a week, Shorty was there on the corner at Mr. Sam's house chopping that stove wood. I mean he chopped a huge pile.

All four of those boys finally made, as far as I know, good citizens. Shorty spent 20 years in the U.S. Army. They all learned the lesson that the boys who went along were companions in crime. They all shared the guilt of those who instigated the crime.

Now to what we are talking about today. The Bible teaches us of the evils of the tongue. In our lesson text, James says, "If any man among you seem to be religious, and bridleth not his tongue, but deceiveth his own heart, this man's religion is vain." The gift of speech is such a wonderful gift of God. Some of the great Roman scholars said that God has distinguished us from the beasts of the field in no greater way than giving us the power of speech. That little instrument we call the voice box is more complicated, marvelous and wonderful than any spaceship this nation has ever made. How wonderful that we can communicate. Yet the tongue can be turned to evil purposes.

James says it is like a little match that starts a fire, and all of hell is on fire (James 3:6). So much evil is done. There are six things that the Lord hates according to the Bible. Yea, seven are an abomination in His sight. One of them is a lying tongue (Proverbs 6:16,17). It is tragic when we develop a dirty mouth and an evil tongue. Blasphemy has always been wrong. Gossip has always been wrong. Character assassination has always been wrong. To use this great gift of God in a way that is evil is tragic indeed.

You know there is something else just as bad — that is the evil ear. Of course the ability to hear is a great and wonderful blessing. I thank God that you and I have the privilege of hearing. It is wonderful to be able to hear. But an evil ear is like an evil tongue. They are companions in crime. It won't do me any good to gossip unless I have that evil ear to listen to my evil tongue. Have you ever thought about that?

We can control what we hear as well as what we say to a great extent.

In the article that I mentioned in the beginning of this lesson, Frank Cox said a preacher in Texas moved to a little town. A good sister in the congregation came over to see the preacher's wife. The first thing she did was to start gossiping about people in that town, talking negative, and telling things uncomplimentary. When she started, the preacher's wife said, "Now wait just a minute. I don't want to hurt your feelings, but I'm not going to listen to that. I don't listen to gossip. I'm not interested in evil. I'm not interested in dirt that someone, maybe unfortunately, was guilty of 10 years ago. If you have anything good to say, if you have anything positive to say, if you have anything of good report, I'll be glad to listen, but I am not going to listen to that." They lived in that town five years. There was never another woman who came to share an evil tongue with that preacher's wife.

You know, it takes one to know one. An evil tongue has to have a companion in crime — an evil ear. The Bible talks about itching ears. Paul told Timothy in 2 Timothy 4:3: "The time will come when they will not endure sound doctrine; but after their own lusts shall they heap to themselves teachers, having itching ears." How true that is when it comes to evil.

I can remember one time making a visit when I was a young minister. A lady said, "You know, we went to visit a certain family. Our little boy opened a dresser drawer, and he saw a deck of cards." Then she turned to my wife and said, "What would you have done?" My wife said, "I would have spanked that kid for meddling. That is what I would have done." You know, we lived in that town for several years and that very lady never opened her mouth with anything evil again.

Now I'll tell you, this evil tongue has to have an evil ear. If you are always hearing something bad, you better take stock. Maybe you have itching ears. The Bible says in Mark 4:24: "Take heed what ye hear." We can control what we hear as well as what we say to a great extent.

Speak a word of praise this week. To give praise is more creative and inspiring than to receive it.

I don't have to listen to filth and trash and blasphemy. The Bible also says in Luke 8:18: "Take heed therefore how you hear." The ability to hear and the ability to talk are great and wonderful blessings of God, our Father, and should be used right.

There are so many good things we can do and say. There are so many people who need a word of encouragement. Would you use your tongue this week to speak a word of encouragement? Do you know some man who is blue and downhearted and who needs a pat on the back? He needs someone to say a word of encouragement.

J.P. Sanders, former dean at David Lipscomb College in Nashville and Pepperdine University in Malibu, California, told me one time about when he was a freshman in college. He said, "I made a good grade in chemistry, and my professor came up to me and said a word of encouragement. Because of that word of encouragement, I majored in the field of chemistry. The encouragement that came to me as a young man determined my whole major in college."

Oh, let us speak a word of encouragement this week. Speak a word of praise this week. To give praise is more creative and inspiring than to receive it. Speak a word of appreciation. Speak a word of sympathy and comfort and cheer. Let's listen for something good this week. Let's listen for something that is beautiful this week. Let's listen for something pure this week. Let's listen for something profitable this week. Let's beware of those companions in crime: The evil tongue and the evil ear.

∾

Madison Church of Christ
Amazing Grace Bible Class
Madison, Tennessee
June 2, 1974

Let Brotherly Love Continue: Does Charity Begin in Your Home?

I have been working for several weeks with the subject "Does Charity Begin in Your Home?" It may not be ripe, but I'm going to share the lesson with you today from our beautiful text: "Let brotherly love continue" (Hebrews 13:1). Ours is a needy world, just as needy today as it was 2,000 years ago when the Savior was born in a barn over in Bethlehem. It doesn't take special brains, special insight, special information or a computer to know that the world is filled with needy people. Poverty, hunger, disease and loneliness are common companions in this world of ours, but they ought never to be accepted as what ought to be. They ought always to be seen as intruders as invaders, not as what should be or what ought to be.

Complacency toward a world in need must never be our attitude. It is so easy to become complacent. It is so easy to become callous. It is so easy to become judgmental. No wonder the Hebrew writer said, "Let brotherly love continue" and added that we must not neglect to show hospitality to strangers (verse 2).

Then he wrote, "Remember them that are in bonds [prison], as bound with them; and them which suffer adversity, as being yourselves also in the body" (verse 3). In regard to prisoners, we hear sayings like this: "Well, they deserve what has happened to them. If they weren't so lazy, they wouldn't be so poor. Serves them right considering the way they live." Have you ever heard statements like that? Now, at times this analysis may be correct, but such judgements are always wrong. Even when the analysis is right, the statement is wrong because it shows a lack of compassion. It shows a lack of concern. It shows the wrong kind of attitude.

They couldn't understand why I preached the love of Jesus Christ, the fatherhood of God, the brotherhood of man, the deity of Christ, the Resurrection.

It is so hard in the church of Christ for us to learn not to be judgmental. When I came to Madison 20 years ago, we met in a little basement. We had a wonderful group of people. There were a few in East Nashville who just couldn't understand why I wasn't judgmental in my preaching. They wanted to tell me how to preach. They wanted me to "take the hide off of everybody and rub the salt in." They wanted Brother Ira North to be the judge of a little handful of people. They couldn't understand why I preached the love of Jesus Christ, the fatherhood of God, the brotherhood of man, the deity of Christ, the Resurrection. They couldn't understand why I knew nothing save Jesus Christ and Him crucified.

I want to tell you right now, we humans are a pretty sorry lot when it comes to judging. We are weak, we are frail, and we are made of dust. "Judge not, that ye be not judged. For with what judgment ye judge, ye shall be judged: and with what measure ye mete, it shall be measured to you again" (Matthew 7:1-2). What the world needs is not a lot of judgmental preaching, but a lot of the love of God our Father, the love of the Lord Jesus Christ. So I'm not surprised that this great text says, "Let brotherly love continue."

I want to suggest that the place for love to begin is at home. Does charity begin in your home?

Notice three commands in this text. The first command is to let brotherly love continue. The second command is to not neglect to show hospitality to strangers. The third command is to remember those who are in prison and those who are ill treated (Hebrews 13:1-3).

We have heard all our lives that "charity begins at home." That is a wise point. That is right. "Charity begins at home" ought to mean that our homes become centers of service — stations of concern — where there is brotherly love, an outreach for strangers, and an unbelievable concern for those who are ill-treated and suffering. That is the thrust of our lesson today. Let me think with you a moment about it. Let us look at these three commands from Hebrews 13 one at a time.

The first is, "Let brotherly love continue." I want us to get a picture like it was 2,000 years ago. I think the Bible is so much more meaningful when we take the time to study the context and the circumstance. In fact anything out of context is very dangerous. One of the first things taught in our Christian colleges about studying the Bible is that a text out of context is a pretext. For example, the Bible says, "There is no God." But when you put the phrase in context — when you put it in the right environment or setting — it means something completely different. Here it is in context: "The fool hath said in his heart, There is no God" (Psalm 14:1). See what difference it makes. It makes all the difference in the world.

A man told me one time, "Some of the happiest days and moments of my life were spent in the arms of another man's wife." I said, "You old lustful rascal." He paused a minute and said, "The arms of my mother." What if I told only the first part of that statement at the barber shop? Wouldn't that be something? The truth comes out only when put the whole story in context.

I want us to consider the circumstances surrounding the Hebrews text. Two thousand years ago the Bible says, in 1 Thessalonians 1:9-10, that people turned to God from serving idols. But it is also true that sometimes when people heard Paul, Barnabas, John or Silas preach, just one family member obeyed the Gospel and believed in Christ. When this happened, there were dire results. Christian converts were ostracized from their family. They were cut off from their jobs.

I remember one time I was teaching a class at David Lipscomb College, and a young German girl was in my Bible class. Somebody said something about sacrificing — oh, how this person had sacrificed. This German student said, "Dr. North, they know nothing about sacrifice." Then she said, "Let me tell you what happened when I obeyed the Gospel. Number one, I was fired from my job. Number two, I was kicked out of my house. My family disinherited me. Number three, I lost every friend I had."

They learned that the ties from the blood of Jesus ... turned out to be stronger than those fleshly ties.

That is the way it was in New Testament times. That is the way it is today. In Italy, I talked to a former priest who had been baptized. He said, "Brother North, the first thing that happened when I was baptized is that my family disinherited me. I went to work the next day, and my employer told me that some of the religious powers had called him. He really hated to, but he said, 'Man, I can't use you.' " He said, "I lost every friend I had."

That is what happened in New Testament times. Many times when a man obeyed the Gospel, his lifeline — socially, emotionally and financially — was completely gone. But an amazing thing happened 2,000 years ago: Christians found out that when they lost their family, their jobs, and their friends, members of the church opened up their hearts and homes, took them in and loved them as their very own. They learned that the ties from the blood of Jesus — the fact that they were members of the church and brothers and sisters in the Lord — turned out to be stronger than those fleshly ties.

You know, we think that blood is thicker than water. Well, blood may be thicker than water, but I'll tell you one thing: There is no blood as powerful as the blood of Jesus that makes us all clean and in Christ Jesus.

So the amazing thing of the pagan world was when someone would obey the Gospel and be ostracized, kicked out of his family, lose his social and financial ties, yet there was another family to love him and to care for him. Now when you see that context and that picture, I think you can understand what Hebrews 13:1 is talking about. The Greek language called this new relationship *phileo,* which means brotherly love. Let increasing familiarity breed concern and not contempt. "Let brotherly love continue."

Does charity begin in your home? Where better on earth for this biblical principal to be than in the Christian family? Is there someone you could enlarge the circle of your family to include? To put in your plan? Is there someone you could open your home and your heart to and to whom you could show this brotherly love?

Do you know why many a person has walked down this aisle and confessed Christ and been baptized? A lot of people don't understand this. There have been hundreds baptized in that baptistery right there because they first experienced the greatness of brotherly love in the context of your home, your zone, your Sunday school class. Or someone visited them in the hospital and showed them Christian people care. We have a basket dinner and someone invites a lonely person who is not a Christian. Here is something different; here is something beautiful; here is something wonderful. He feels he is loved not because of what he has. It makes no difference if he has nothing, but he is loved because of what he can become through Jesus Christ. So where better on earth could it begin than in the home?

> *"Charity begins at home" ought to mean that our homes become centers of service — stations of concern.*

The second command in Hebrews 13 deals with a love for strangers. We must put this in context. The early Christians extended their love to everybody in the church, including those who had been ostracized when they obeyed the Gospel. They also extended the same love to strangers. When these evangelists and people were traveling around, they didn't have a Ramada Inn. They didn't have nice hotels. Even I can remember when it was a problem to travel. I can remember going to Texas and looking for a tourist home, where you just stayed in somebody's home. It is hard for us to understand how just a few years ago travel was a problem. I want you to remember strangers, said the writer. Where better for this hospitality to be shown than in the home?

In our day and time many of us are living in small apartments on 50-foot lots. We sometimes don't have room for company. Yet the need for the fellowship that the New Testament writer is talking about is as

great today as ever, maybe greater than it has ever
been in the history of the world. The loneliest place
on earth can be the big city. It won't be long before
90 percent of us in America will live in cities. The
small farm is disappearing. People are going to cities
by the hundreds of thousands every year. We are all
going to be city folks. Some of the loneliest places on
earth are the Loop in Chicago or Times Square in
New York. One Christian lady said when I asked
why she was so gracious, "Well, my father entertains
strangers in our home. He talks to salesmen and just
anybody who comes along. One time I said, 'Dad,
why are you so interested in getting acquainted with
people?' My father gave a reply that was profound,
and I never forgot. He said, 'Darling daughter, you'll
never meet anyone who is not lonely.' "

*Let increasing familiarity breed
concern and not contempt. "Let
brotherly love continue."*

The Madison Church has five fellowship rooms.
They are used almost 365 days a year. We are fixing
to add a sixth. By the grace of God, in a few days we
will have open the most beautiful fellowship room
you have ever seen, with a stainless steel kitchen
that is out of this world. I want to plead with us to
use it like we use these that we already have. When
new members come in and people come who are not
members of the church, I want us to show them hospitality. It makes no difference how they dress. It
makes no difference where they work. It makes no
difference if they have a Ph.D. or if they can't read

or write their name. Let us be kind and let us be gracious. Let us show love to strangers. We cannot be afraid to take a chance.

I heard Marshal Keeble make the finest point. He said, "Thank God the apostle doesn't live today. My brethren would never take a chance on a man like Saul." Saul of Tarsus was a murderer. Sometimes we don't even welcome an ex-convict. Sometimes we don't even want a prostitute who wants to do better and turn from sin and come be one of us. Saul was the chief of sinners. Here was a man who made havoc with the church of God. Jesus Christ took a chance on him. And as Marshal Keeble points out, he became the greatest preacher the world has ever known. God chose him to write most of the New Testament, most of the 27 books. So I say, let us in our own homes and in our own hearts and in our own lives not be afraid to show hospitality. Let love for strangers continue.

One of our members, who is sitting here right now, bought an automobile agency in a small Middle Tennessee town, but he said, "I lived there about four years and sold out and left." I said "Why?" He said, "I never could break in. My father didn't come over on the Mayflower. I was ostracized." I said, "You mean Lawrenceburg, Mount Pleasant, Columbia and Lewisburg are clannish?" He said, "The most clannish places on earth." I said, "I never did know it." "Yeah," he said, "But where was your great-grandfather from?" I said, "All Lawrence County celebrated his birthday. He was there 50 years. My great-grandfather, my grandfather, my father and me. I was always accepted." He said,

"Yeah, you were, but you ought to move across one of those county lines and see how long it will take you to break in." Isn't that something?

You know, teenagers can be clannish too. We have the sweetest group of young people. But young people, did you know that teenagers can be clannish? I've had young people tell me, "Man, these are clannish teenagers, I'm on the outside, and they won't let me in." We don't want that at Madison, do we? We don't even want it in our own homes.

The family who makes love its way of life discovers great things.

Then last command in our text from Hebrews 13 is to have a love for the needy. Remember those who are in prison as though you are in prison with them. Remember those who are ill-treated since you are in the body. We are all frail. Oh, we can suffer so easily. We need to remember with special care those who are suffering. It could happen to us. I think about that every time announcements are made at church. You could be in the hospital with cancer tomorrow. You could lose your wife or your husband or the nearest, dearest person to you today. The person you love better than life could be at the funeral home in a coffin tonight at 9 o'clock. It could happen to any of us. And so we are commanded to remember when one is in prison. You know people were thrown in prison for being Christians in New Testament days. You remember somebody who was ill-treated because that person is in the body; it could happen to you.

The family who makes love its way of life discovers great things. When it reaches out to the oppressed, it links us with the love of God. Don't you forget: When we were distressed and in despair Christ Jesus died for us. Someone has said that charity began in God's house but it did not end there. We do not want it to end there. Does charity begin in your home? Does brotherly love reign in your house? Does love for strangers rule in your house? Is there love for the needy at your house?

Let us pray. Oh, loving, heavenly Father, we can see the big ways to love, the dramatic ways. Would You show us the little ways? Would You keep us loving when we want to quit? Would You nudge our love to reach out further when we are tempted to love only the attractive? Would You forgive us if we have been more concerned about teaching our children how to learn to spell and do arithmetic or play baseball than we are in teaching them concern for others? If manners at our house have become more important than kindness, would You forgive us? If polite speech has been stressed more at our house than we have stressed gracious deeds and involvement for Christ, would You forgive us? Would You let us in our little family circles here at Madison, each one of us, practice these three great principles given us in the Hebrew letter? We pray this for family here at Madison, this church of Christ on this corner. Would You let us always show brotherly love? Let brotherly love continue here, Lord. Let love for strangers show. Don't let us become cold and clannish; don't let us try to cut anyone out. Oh God, let us have great love for the needy. Let us be more interested in showing mercy than in judging. Keep us close together and close to You. For we pray in the name of Jesus the Christ, Amen.

∾

Madison Church of Christ
Madison, Tennessee
June 4, 1972

The Bible: Our Only Guide

I like to talk about the Bible. I thank God we have an infallible guide. It is so wonderful in this old sin-cursed earth that we have something safe, solid, sound and sure.

I held a meeting in West Palm Beach, Florida, a few years ago and went out to fish with Captain Haynes. He had a marvelous boat. He took us out, and we got out so far I couldn't see the land. A storm came up, and I was a little frightened. I went up on the bow of the boat, and I said, "Captain Haynes, I believe we are going in the wrong direction. I believe we are going farther out in the ocean." He said, "Brother North, do you see that?" He pointed to the compass, and I said, "Yes, I see it." He said, "That is my Bible out here, and the compass says we are going right. I've been out here many times and felt like you do now — that we are turned around and going the wrong way. But that compass has never failed to bring me safely home. You use that in a sermon someday." I said, "I will Sunday — if I live." I was glad to finally see the shore. Where I was raised, you were not afraid of water as long as you could see both banks at the same time.

We need to believe the Bible, we need to love the Bible, and we need to live the Bible.

I want to make three simple suggestions about the Holy Bible: We need to believe the Bible, we need to love the Bible, and we need to live the Bible. First, we need to believe the Bible. I do believe the Bible with all of my heart and with all of my soul. I am willing to stake everything that I am or ever hope to be on the truthfulness of the Word of God. I can tell you a lot of reasons why I believe the Bible, but I want to mention three simple ones that I think are unquestionable.

A great American statesman said to take all the Bible you can by reason, the rest by faith and you'll live a better life and die a better death. I believe the Bible because it cannot be destroyed. Anyone familiar with the history of the Bible knows Satan has tried to burn it out, laugh it out, and reason it out. But it is still here.

The other day I was trying to give a psychologist the biblical view on homosexuality and lesbianism. This psychologist shrugged her shoulders and said, "Oh, in just a few years we'll look back and laugh at the position against homosexuals. It will be accepted like so many things." This reminds me of the prediction that in 50 years people will be so smart you will have to go to a museum to even see a Bible. The very printing press on which that blasphemy was printed was later used to print Bibles. More than fifty years have passed by and the Bible is the largest selling book in the world. You can't burn it out; can't laugh it out; can't reason it out. I don't know what the future holds, but I know one thing: The Word is going to be here, for "Heaven and earth shall pass away, but my words shall not pass away" (Matthew 24:35).

I believe the Bible with all my heart because it is always up to date. Isn't it unbelievable how things get out of date? Publishers tell me they cannot get textbooks off the printing press fast enough to keep them up to date. They are out of date when they roll off the press. Biology books that are 25 years old are not worth a dime. A medical book a hundred years old is a joke. I'll tell you one book that is as new as tomorrow's newspaper — that is the book I hold in my hand, the Bible.

One time I said to Brother Gus Nichols, whom I love and appreciate so much, "Well, Brother Gus, how long have you been down here in Jasper, Alabama?" He said, "Just 42 years." I said, "Brother Gus, aren't you scraping the bottom of the barrel for ideas? Haven't you really run out of sermon material?" Brother Gus said, "Brother North, there are 10,000 more sermons in there that I haven't preached yet, and I want to live to preach them every one in Jasper, Alabama." That is what I tell them at Madison, Tennessee, if anybody ever suggests we ought to change preachers: "Wait a minute. Woah! I've got 10,000 more sermons left."

I believe the Bible because from "In the beginning" in Genesis to the last "Amen" in Revelation there is not a single contradiction. The harmony of the Bible is unbelievable: one central theme — salvation of man; one central personality — the Lord Jesus Christ. How are you going to explain that? How did a group of ignorant fishermen, who never saw the inside of a college, just accidentally get together and write such a book? Isn't it easier to just believe? It is 10,000 times easier to believe than it is to disbelieve, if your mind is open and your heart is receptive.

Now I had a professor one time at the University of Illinois who made fun of the Bible. And I just suggested, "Why don't some of you fellows who think the Bible was written by a group of ignorant fishermen and farmers, not inspired of God, why don't you get together and write one better?" You know I would rather have the copyright on a book better than the Bible than own all the oil fields in West Texas. I guarantee you one thing, if the university professors could do it, you better believe they would do it. The truth of it is, if you got 40 of them together, not only would they have a book with 4,011 contradictions, but I'll bet you a betcha (and all I ever bet is a betcha) there wouldn't any two of them agree. Yet here we have the Holy Bible, book divine, that is completely consistent. How marvelous and wonderful. Believe the Bible.

My second point is to love the Bible. We ought to have a great affection for the Word of God. We ought to love it enough not to add to it or take from it. I know that is written in the book of Revelation, but it applies to every book in the Bible. "For I testify unto every man that heareth the words of the prophecy of this book, If any man shall add unto these things, God shall add unto him the plagues that are written in this book: And if any man shall take away from the words of the book of this prophecy, God shall take away his part out of the book of life, and out of the holy city, and from the things which are written in this book" (Revelation 22:18-19). You ought to love the Bible enough to preach the gospel of Christ just as it is revealed in the New Testament. "But though we, or an angel from heaven, preach any other gospel unto you than that which we have preached unto you, let him be accursed. As we said before, so say I now again, If any man preach any other gospel unto you than that ye have received, let him be accursed" (Galatians 1:8-9).

We ought to have a great affection for the Word of God. We ought to love it enough not to add to it or take from it.

We ought to love the Bible enough to contend earnestly for its truths. I'd lots rather somebody else do it, but I have made it a practice in the little community where I live that when the media calls me and says, "Brother North, we want a statement," I agree to give one. They ask, "Will you do it on camera?" I say, "Yes, I'll do it on camera. Bring the cameras out. Set them up." I believe you ought to love the Bible enough to speak up. You know we may be misunderstood; there may be a little criticism. That won't hurt you. I've learned this at Madison. A little criticism does you good.

We never reach the point where we do not need to open the Bible with an open mind and study it.

When Mrs. North and I were educating all our children — you know it is rough when you've got three in college at the same time since these colleges won't give an examination until you pay the tuition — I'd call our elders together and I'd get some bulletin that had given a pretty good discussion of me. I'd say, "This is what some folks think about your preacher" and let them read it. I could see the redness coming up and finally one of them would say, "I just recommend that we give Brother North a nice big raise." Rain from heaven. I needed that so badly with all those kids. A little criticism is not going to hurt you as long as you are contending earnestly for the faith and upholding the Word of God. Sometimes it might just help.

I believe we ought to love the Bible enough to study it. I don't think a man gets too old to study the Bible. The man who taught me that truth was the most powerful classroom teacher I ever had. I never saw anyone at Louisiana State University, Vanderbilt, Peabody or University of Illinois who could match him. He taught me that as long as there is life, there is danger. The devil never gives up. The devil never quits. He is always after you. When we studied the book of Genesis and came to Noah after the flood, he made us memorize the saying, "As long as there is life there is danger." It breaks my heart tonight that he has left the faith and left the church, because that great principle he taught me is true. We never reach the point where we do not need to open the Bible with an open mind and study it.

We ought to love the Bible enough to meditate on it. I just preached the funeral of an 80-year-old man who had been a deacon at Madison for about 35 years. He loved to meditate on the Bible. When I think of him, I always think about Psalm 1:2 "But his delight is in the law of the Lord; and in his law doth he meditate day and night." I'm told that Brother David Lipscomb in his last years was almost blind. He would sit on his front porch there on the campus with the Bible open on his lap, even though he was unable to read. Sometimes some of the students would come by and notice that Brother David had his Bible upside-down. But he had read it so often and knew it so well he could meditate on the Word of God even though he could not see to read it. I want to love the Bible like that — deeply, sincerely, from the depth of my heart.

The third suggestion that I want to make about the Bible is that we live it by example. The most powerful form of teaching is example. That is why those of us who are preachers of the Word have to make an honest, sincere, conscientious effort to live it. A lot of people do not pay as much attention as they should to what we say, but they read our lives clearly.

I have thought back, "What was it that made me believe as a child that the church was the most important thing on earth? What taught me that heaven-born, blood-bought institution, the church of my Lord, is the grandest, greatest, sweetest, finest, most marvelous thing on earth?" It was my father. You know it wasn't so much what Dad said. Dad was just a small-town business man. It was what Dad did. We never missed services of the church, not one time in my life. Nobody ever asked, "Are we going to attend services today?" If the door was open, we were going to be there — rain, sleet or snow. Not one time in my life did Dad ever say, "It is snowing, it is sleeting, the wind is blowing. Are we going to attend service?" Dad didn't say much, except by the life he lived. He practiced his faith in every decision he made in business. Don't tell me that a man can't make a living and be honest. I know he can. I saw my dad make decisions, always asking, "Is it right? What about the church? Will this help the church? Will this put the church in a favorable light?" I plead with our young fathers and mothers to rear their children like that. I tell you one thing; A man can't live long enough to forget an example like that.

There is a character in the Bible that I think of when I preach on example. I think of a young man who set such a great example for all of us and for the youth of all ages. When he was 17, he was sold as a slave. You know some of us think we have a bad break. We think, "Well, looks like they have dealt us a terrible hand." What if you were sold as a slave when you were 17? What about that? This man was sold as a slave by his own blood brothers. It hurts to be betrayed, but to be betrayed by your own family is something else. To be betrayed by your own brothers and sisters in Christ can be devastating. Here is a young man sold into slavery because of those green-eyed monsters, envy and jealousy. The same monsters took Jesus to the cross. It can take a preacher to Hell. It can cause us to do so much harm. Yet in spite of all of that evil done to him, this clean young man — not one ugly word in all the Bible ever was said about Joseph — he remained loyal and faithful and true.

Then Joseph had another experience that I think was just as devastating. He was thrown in prison by a conniving, lying, scheming woman, because he would not yield to her advances. You say, "Well, that doesn't happen today." Yes, it does happen today, and it is awful. Judge Sam Davis Tatum — a distinguished juvenile judge in Tennessee who had tried about 15,000 cases and was a faithful member of the church — told me before he died: "I was on the bench one day trying a case and a young woman about 19 or 20 years of age came up afterward. She said, 'Judge, do you remember a few years ago defending a man that was sent to the penitentiary for life for molesting a little girl?' I thought a minute and said, 'I sure do remember that case. Why?' She looked him in the eye and said, 'Judge, I am that little girl.' She said, 'That man never touched me. I told on that stand exactly what my mother told me to say. My mother hated him with a purple passion and there wasn't anything she wouldn't do to put him away.'" Judge Tatum said that hit him in the face like a cold towel. He immediately got his files and did further investigation and turned up more evidence. He walked into the governor's office and said, "Governor McCord, there is an innocent man out here at the state penitentiary serving a life sentence because of a vicious and tragic lie." Governor Jim McCord pardoned that man.

I can't imagine a tougher blow than that like Joseph endured. When in prison he made a good slave, as every follower of God our Father ought to do. Do the best you can whatever the circumstances. Then they forgot him. We all know the end of the story. He became prime minister of Egypt. I love the story of Joseph. If Joseph could remain true under those circumstances, I don't care if we do live in a materialistic, godless, atheistic world, we can still seek truth.

We have the greatest example the world has ever known — Jesus the Christ. I'm so glad I can say to you not only to do what the Savior says but do what the Savior did. It is so easy, for example, for me to speak on forgiveness. I like to preach on forgiveness. Isn't it wonderful to be redeemed, to be forgiven, to have everything you have ever thought, said and done wrong gone forever? It is just marvelous.

Three simple suggestions: read the Bible; love the Bible; exemplify the Bible. Thank God we have a guide.

I tell people the reason I want them to obey the Gospel is the joy of being new in Christ and being forgiven. Jesus said to forgive even your enemies. That is pretty easy to preach, but we see our blessed Lord on the cross doing it. Here He is the purest man ever lived. He has been misrepresented; He has been falsely accused; He is dying the most ignominious death the world has ever known. Jesus the Son of God — the man who opened the eyes of the blind, caused the lame to walk, the deaf to hear, and lived the greatest life the world has ever known. Leaving the shining courts of heaven, my old brethren used to say, "Born in a barn for you and me." What did He say? He showed no hostility, no bitterness. He lived perfectly the teachings that He gave us and prayed for His persecutors, forgiveness. I love Jesus as the example. "Jesus, Jesus, Jesus, sweetest name I know." I like to preach the sweet story of Jesus. "Tell me the story of Jesus, sweetest ever heard."

Three simple suggestions: read the Bible; love the Bible; exemplify the Bible. Thank God we have a guide.

∾

Spiritual Sword Lectureship
Memphis, Tennessee
January, 1970

What Must I Do To Be Saved?

Let's read Acts 16:25-33: "And at midnight Paul and Silas prayed, and sang praises unto God: and the prisoners heard them. And suddenly there was a great earthquake, so that the foundations of the prison were shaken: and immediately all the doors were opened, and every one's bands were loosed. And the keeper of the prison awaking out of his sleep, and seeing the prison doors open, he drew out his sword, and would have killed himself, supposing that the prisoners had been fled. But Paul cried with a loud voice, saying, Do thyself no harm: for we are all here. Then he called for a light, and sprang in, and came trembling, and fell down before Paul and Silas, And brought them out, and said, Sirs, what must I do to be saved? And they said, Believe on the Lord Jesus Christ, and thou shalt be saved, and thy house. And they spake unto him the word of the Lord, and to all that were in his house. And he took them the same hour of the night, and washed their stripes; and was baptized, he and all his, straightway."

My friends, there was a time in the churches of Christ when most of the preaching we heard was on what we call first principles. I remember as a boy in the little congregation at Ethridge where I was reared, we had preaching once a month and nearly all the sermons were on what we called first principles: "What to do to be saved." I think that was a tragic mistake. We never had a sermon on self-righteousness. We never had a sermon on prejudice. We were spiritually under-nourished. We were so far from really practicing the Golden Rule. Yet we thought we were the chosen of God. It never dawned on us to examine how weak, poor and lowly we were. I think, maybe in reaction to that, we have erred in the other direction and not really given pulpit time to the great, primary principles of the Gospel of Jesus Christ.

I am very pleased when I see an interest in religion anywhere. I do believe that some religion is better than no religion. We must keep our bearings and always remember that the Bible is the Word of God, and that no question is answered right until it is answered scripturally and biblically.

I want us to analyze this morning probably the most important question in all the world: What must I do to be saved? I want us to take it word by word, phrase by phrase, and think about it. We will start at the very end of the question and come back to the first.

"What must I do to be *saved*?" What does it mean to be saved? People ask, "Are you saved, brother?" I'm glad to hear people asking that. What is it to be saved? Well, to be saved is to be forgiven of everything you have ever thought, said or done that is wrong, that is contrary to the will of God Almighty. It is so wonderful to be forgiven.

I remember a story told by a preacher: "I had a brother who was older than I was. He was sickly and small, and I was always big and strong. Sometimes, because I was much stronger than my brother, I picked on him. Though he was older, I could whip him. My physical prowess was great. One day I was picking on him and my mother walked in just as I had hauled off and slapped my brother real hard. I will never, never forget the look on my mother's face when she saw me do that. My conscience hurt me all day long. I asked Mother if she wanted me to sweep the floor. She would say, 'No.' 'Do you want me to bring in the wood?' 'No.' 'Do you want me to go to the store for you?' 'No.' Finally, as the day wore on, it was just more than I could stand. I walked in the kitchen and put my arms around her, dropped to my knees, and wept. I said, 'Mama, it was a cowardly and terrible thing for me to do; please forgive me. I'll never, never do it again.' To which Mother said, 'You are forgiven; it is all in the past, and it will never be mentioned again.' "

It is a wonderful thing to be forgiven of all trespasses. To be saved is to have all the sins and mistakes of the past gone forever. To be saved is to be freed and redeemed from the most terrible form of slavery the world has ever known. In this great land of ours, we don't know what it is to be a slave or, to be beaten like a dog, whipped, controlled completely, body and soul. I think of the days of slavery in our own country as one of the saddest times. How could a preacher of the Gospel try to justify slavery? But, you know, some of them tried to do it. Now we say, "My, my, how could they?"

When I was living in Baton Rouge, we visited New Orleans and went on a tour with Howard White. At that time he was the minister of the Carrollton Avenue Church. I will never forget going through the French Quarter and to the Old Slave Market. He pointed out a block where they used to strip human beings and sell them on that block like an animal.

He told me a true story. One time a man from the North, who had never seen a human being sold, came down to New Orleans. He was dressed in a white suit. He was a rich man. He saw a young man stripped and put on the block. The man was strong, handsome and fine looking. The auctioneer said, "What am I bid for this man? Perfect health, strong with many years of work ahead. Who will start the bidding at one thousand dollars?" One man said "A thousand dollars." "Who'll make it twelve?" "Twelve hundred." "He is worth more than that. Who'll make it fifteen?" A voice in the crowd said, "Two thousand dollars for the man." The auctioneer banged his gavel and said, "Sold, to the man in the white suit." The man came up and wrote a check for $2,000, got the papers, turned them over, endorsed them, went over to the young black man, and said, "Son you are a free man; you have been redeemed and here are your papers to prove it." The slave dropped to his knees and said, "Sir, I'll serve you the rest of my life. I never saw such unselfishness; I never dreamed that such love existed in the universe. I didn't know that there was a man who had a heart with such compassion and care." The man in the white suit said, "Get up! I said you are redeemed. You do not have to serve anybody. You are a free man. I have paid the price, and here are your papers."

If a man redeemed you like that wouldn't you love him forever? To be saved is to be redeemed from a bondage more cruel, from the power and guilt of sin. To be saved is to be in right relationship with God, the Father and Creator of the universe. It is to be an heir of God. What would you give today to be an heir of the Rockefeller fortune or the Kennedy fortune or the DuPont fortune? What would you give? Yet all of us in this auditorium could be heirs to something a hundred thousand times, yea a hundred million times greater than any man-made fortune. We can be a joint heir with the Son of God. To be saved is to be a child of God, a sharer of the eternal, abundant inheritance of Jesus Christ.

Yes, it is a wonderful thing to be saved. To be saved is to be clean on the inside. Aren't you glad that you live in a land where there is plenty of water and soap? Isn't it wonderful also after a hard day's work to take a good bath and be clean? Doesn't it make you feel good to put on clean clothes and know that they are clean? But there is something a hundred times better, and that is to be clean on the inside.

I never shall forget holding a meeting at the Granny White Church a few years ago. At the close of one service, a young woman came up and said, "I need to talk to you a few minutes." She told me some of her problems and heartaches. I said, "Why don't you think seriously tonight and come back tomorrow night and do something about it?" She said, "No, I don't want to wait till tomorrow night. I feel so dirty on the inside." I went out into the hall and asked Sister Chumley to assist the young woman for baptism right then. The young woman and I waded out in the water and I baptized her. When she came up out of the water, I said, "Sue, there is one thing for sure: You are going home clean tonight on the inside."

To be saved is to be forgiven; to be redeemed; to be right with God; to be a brother of Jesus Christ; to be a child of the King; to be in a covenant relation to God. That is what being saved means.

Now, let's take the next word, "do": "What must I *do* to be saved?"

In the religious world we have forgotten that faith that is not obedient can never save. James says, "Shew me thy faith without thy works, and I will shew thee my faith by my works" (James 2:18). In other words, "You show me your faith without obedience, and I'll show you my faith by obedience." He said (paraphrased), "You say to a brother 'be warm and filled' but you don't give him anything to wear and you don't give him anything to eat. What good does it do? It does none" (v. 16, 17).

Then he says in James 2:19, "The devils also believe, and tremble." The devil knows that Jesus is the Son of God. The devil knows that God is the true and living God. He knows it, and he trembles. The devil has what we call historical faith. But I'll tell you one thing: he doesn't intend to submit himself to the will and to the Word of almighty God.

The Lord said in the greatest and the most famous sermon ever preached, "Not everyone that saith unto me, Lord, Lord, shall enter into the kingdom of heaven; but he that doeth the will of my Father which is in heaven" (Matthew 7:21).

I'm not opposed to emotion in Christianity. How are you going to rule out emotion? People say they live without emotion. Nonsense. I don't object to some emotion, but I have never encouraged a lot of whooping and shouting because I don't believe it gets a man one inch closer to heaven.

In the religious world we have forgotten that faith that is not obedient can never save.

What I want to encourage is doing the will of God: "Not every one that saith unto me Lord, Lord, shall enter into the kingdom of heaven; but he that doeth the will of my Father in heaven." Blessed are they who do His commandments that they may have a right to the tree of life and enter in through the gate into the city. The religion of Jesus isn't something you get; it is not an experience that you have somewhere or something supernatural that swoops down and shakes you and you see a light. It is a rational religion. It is a religion of great feeling, but it is a religion of obedience.

So the great question is, "What must I do?" There is something to do. It doesn't mean that you earn it; it doesn't mean that you deserve it. It does mean that obedience has a part in the greatest question the world has ever known.

The third word is "I": "What must *I* do to be saved?" It is an individual thing. Paul says each must give an account of himself to God. Some things

I can't do for you and you can't do for me. I can't confess Christ for you; I can't take the Lord's Supper for you; I can't be baptized for you; I can't answer in the judgment day for you. How many mothers would like to obey for their son? How many wives would like to obey for their husband? How many husbands would like to obey for their wife? How many brothers would like to obey for a sister and how many sisters would like to obey for a brother? There are just some things we cannot do for another.

I think those of us who are parents have to understand that there comes a time when we have to turn loose. There comes a time when we have to cut the apron strings. There comes a time when we have to say, "The boy is grown. I have prayed; I have talked; I have worked; I have done everything I know for him. I must trust God and trust my son because I can't live his life and he can't live mine." There are some things a man has to do for himself. He will have to give account for his own soul at the judgment day, and there isn't anybody in the world who can take his place. The only one who can plead his case successfully is the Lord Jesus Christ.

I'm going to stand before the Lord God Almighty alone. I can't have the Madison church to answer for me. I can't even have these great elders whom I love dearly stand up there with me and back and vouch for me. No, I'm going to walk that lonesome valley, and I'm going to walk it alone. Jesus is going to have to be my advocate. I'm going to stand before God and give an account for my own soul. Christianity is so intensely personal that it is frightening. You say it is wonderful, but it is also frightening.

The fourth word I want us to look at in this great question is "must": "What *must* I do to be saved?" This question is not what *might* I do? When Paul was on the way to Damascus, he saw the Lord. This qualified him to be an apostle, for one had to see Jesus after His resurrection to be qualified to be an apostle. When Paul said he was born out of due season, he was referring to that special act of God that permitted him to be an apostle. He said, "Lord what wilt thou have me to do?" Jesus said, "Go into the city, and it shall be told thee what thou *must* do" (Acts 9:6).

If I say I might do something, it means maybe. But if say I must, I'm talking about what is absolutely essential. This question is, what must you do to be saved, not just what might you do. Tell me what is absolutely necessary beyond a shade of a doubt for me to do to be saved.

Now we come to the first word and the real crux of the question. We have talked about *to be saved*; we have talked about *do*; we have talked about *I*; we have talked about *must*. Now we come to the real crux of the question, *what.*

Ladies and gentlemen, it is such a responsibility to answer this question that I wouldn't for my right arm mislead you. I wouldn't for my right arm just tell you it is something that might be right. James says, "Be not many of you teachers, my brethren, knowing that we shall receive heavier judgement" (James 3:1 ASV). What a responsibility to answer this question. How tragic it would be at the judgment day to find that I had misled people because I had told them something that just absolutely was not right and they were lost.

This question about salvation is asked three times in the book of Acts in Acts 2, Acts 9 and Acts 16. I want us to analyze it, and you will find the same answer all three times. If the question is asked three times and answered alike three times, then I can be sure and you can be sure of the answer. When we are sure, we must stand for it. I want to remind our young people that compromise does not change the truth, and when it comes to this question that has to do with man's eternal destiny, you cannot compromise and you cannot speak what you think, I think or somebody else thinks. We have to contend for what God thinks and what God says.

The question is asked in Acts 16 when Paul and Silas were cast in prison. The Bible says they were in prison at midnight, singing and praying. They had been whipped, which was an unlawful thing for Paul since he was a Roman citizen. You know when they came and told them to leave, Paul said "No. They have beaten us, Roman citizens, uncondemned and without a fair trial. They are going to come and escort us out like gentlemen." He made them do it.

When they were in the prison, they first had been scourged or whipped. Some of those Roman soldiers could wield a lash with unbelievable power. In fact, some of them could crack a whip over a man's back that would cut like a surgeon's knife. I'm sure that one reason our Lord fainted beneath the cross was from the loss of blood from scourging.

So the Roman soldiers had beaten Paul and Silas and thrown them in prison. Not satisfied just to put them in a cell, they put their hands and feet in stocks where they couldn't sit up or lean back and be comfortable. Then came the midnight hour in that dungeon, and something was going on in that prison that the prison had not seen before: a prayer meeting.

I wonder how many of you have ever visited a prison. You ought to visit one sometime. When I was a boy, they gave tours of the state penitentiary. I visited that when I was in the seventh grade. I tell you, that electric chair was the most frightening thing I ever saw. I said, "Lord, if You will be with me, I ain't ever going to come to this place." To see men caged like animals shakes you up. I visited the cells too. I tell you, there is cursing. A jail is a rough, tough, stinking place. Of course officials tell you that they aren't running a country club. The boys are not there for Sunday school.

I can imagine the shock of the prisoners in this story when, instead of all that cursing, these men were praying — not complaining or blaming God, just praying and singing as their backs bled and their hands and feet were in stocks. What an impression that must have made! It was different — how different.

Then at midnight came the great miracle, the earthquake. The doors of that old prison were shaken open. In those days, when a jailer let his prisoner go, he had to give his own life. The jailer summed it up right quick no doubt: "My prisoners are gone. I'll be publicly executed. It will disgrace my family, so I'll just draw my sword, kill myself and spare them the terrible humiliation." As he drew his sword, Paul said, "Do thyself no harm. We are all here; everything is all right" (paraphrased).

Man, that jailer summed up right quick from that answer and that prayer meeting: "Sirs, what must I do to be saved?" Paul said, "Believe on the Lord Jesus Christ, and thou shalt be saved, and thy house."

How sad that nine out of 10 of our wonderful preachers in this country, coast-to-coast, don't read the next verse. I don't know why. Maybe one reason is that money wouldn't roll-in because it is unpopular. People don't want that next verse. How can you believe in someone about whom you have not heard? How can you hear without a preacher? This jailer is a pagan; he doesn't know anything about Jesus. He asks, "What must I do?" Paul answered, "You must believe on Jesus; let me tell you about Jesus." He tells him about Jesus. Did Paul say, "You have to have an experience of grace"? No. What did he do? The Bible says he baptized the jailer the same hour of the night. The jailer heard the sweet story of Jesus, and he was baptized the same hour of the night.

Somebody has said the verse doesn't say that the jailer repented. I'm confident he repented and confessed the Lord, for the Bible says "except ye repent, ye shall all likewise perish" (Luke 13:3). You can't preach Jesus without telling people to turn from their sins. I'm confident he confessed Christ because Romans 10:10 teaches that "with the mouth confession is made unto salvation." You can't preach Christ without preaching that we must confess Him.

The second place our question is asked is in Acts 9 when Saul of Tarsus was on the way to Damascus and the great light shown round about him. He was smitten blind. He said, "What wilt thou have me to do?" Jesus said, "Go into the city, and it shall be told thee what thou must do." When he went in, the gospel preacher was there.

When somebody is saved, there is almost always a gospel preacher. Somebody asks, "Why?" Well, it pleased God through the foolishness of preaching to save those who believe. It pleased the God of heaven to commit the Good News to earthen vessels. So the preacher went to Saul and said (paraphrased), "You believe in Jesus; you've been crying three days and nights; you are sorry for what you have done wrong. Arise and be baptized and wash away your sins, calling on the name of the Lord."

Regardless of how bad you have been or how good you think you are, you need Jesus. You need His gospel and His plan of salvation.

A third time the question was asked was the first time the Gospel — the death, burial and resurrection of our Lord — was preached. In Acts 2 the church was established, and Peter preached the great sermon that said, "You crucified Jesus." So, the people asked, "What shall we do?" (Acts 2:37).

Peter said to those people who heard that sermon and believed Jesus was the Christ, "Repent, and be baptized every one of you in the name of Jesus Christ for the remission of sins, and ye shall receive the gift of the Holy Ghost." Jesus said in John 3:5 that one must be born of the water and the Spirit or you can't enter the kingdom.

Here in Acts 2, Acts 9 and Acts 16 we have people entering the kingdom, the church. What did they do? Dearly beloved, they heard the story of Jesus Christ, and they believed it. They were sorry for their sins and turned from them. They confessed faith in Christ. They were baptized into Christ. And the Lord added them to the church. That is the new birth. That is the scriptural, biblical, unchangeable answer to the greatest question in the world: What must I do to be saved?

It is no compliment to Christ when we tell people: "It is all right; you don't have to turn from sin; you don't have to confess Christ; you don't have to be baptized. Just say you believe and you are saved." Brethren that is not in the Book. That doesn't change anything. It is such an important question. Let us always bear in mind the biblical answer and always hold it up.

If you haven't done what the Bible says, even though you may be the best man in Madison, you may be like Cornelius of Acts 10 — you may be generous and love everybody; you may be loyal and honest. But Cornelius was all of that and he was lost. "Send for Peter to tell you words by which you and your house may be saved" (paraphrased). Peter came in and preached the gospel of Christ and said to the Jews, "Can any man forbid water, that these [Gentiles] should not be baptized?" And he baptized them right there.

Regardless of how bad you have been or how good you think you are, you need Jesus. You need His gospel and His plan of salvation. Would you obey it today?

༄

Amazing Grace Bible Class
Madison, Tennessee
November 5, 1978

Baptism

Today I am discussing an important message and one that I want our young people to know the truth on. Some of us who have been in the church for many years forget that we are baptizing people every week, sometimes every day, at Madison. Many of these have not heard the old-time preachers preach on basic biblical themes. If you have heard sermons about baptism many times before, that is all right. Peter told folks, "Wherefore I will not be negligent to put you always in remembrance of these things, though ye know them, and be established in the present truth" (2 Peter 1:12). So I make no apologies for preaching today on the Biblical theme of baptism.

I'm calling your attention to our text, which is from Matthew 3:11-12 in which John the Baptist is speaking. "I indeed baptize you with water unto repentance: but he that cometh after me is mightier than I, whose shoes I am not worthy to bear: he shall baptize you with the Holy Ghost, and with fire: Whose fan is in his hand, and he will thoroughly purge his floor, and gather his wheat into the garner; but he will burn up the chaff with unquenchable fire."

In this text three baptisms are mentioned: the water baptism unto repentance by John the Baptist; the Holy Spirit baptism; and the baptism of fire. The Bible mentions two more baptisms I want us to talk about today also. One is the baptism of suffering. The other is the baptism of the Great Commission. I think it will help us so much in our religious life and in our understanding of the Word of God to know the truth on these five baptisms.

It is true that we don't have to be baptized but one time, but we want to be sure we have the right baptism that one time, baptism into Jesus.

First, I want to talk about John's baptism. Mark 1:4 says, "John did baptize in the wilderness." That is in the thinly populated areas, in the rural areas. Sometimes today we think of the wilderness as a place of great trees and thickets, or a barren place. But the meaning here is the rural, or outlying, areas. He preached the baptism of repentance for the remission of sins. John preached entirely to the Jewish people, and his baptism was one of repentance for the remission of sins. That is, his baptism grew out of, or followed, repentance. People accepted his baptism in order to have their sins forgiven, to straighten up their life for the coming of the Messiah, Christ Jesus, our Lord. It was immersion and took place very often in the Jordan River.

In 1960 I was in the Bible Lands. Brother Teddlie from Dallas and I took a young Armenian man, about 30 years old, and traveled from Jerusalem to Jericho. We went on to the Jordan River to the place where, according to tradition, Jesus was baptized. We don't know for sure, but there is a place where the guides and historians say John did most of his baptizing. When we got there, it amazed me that one Arab at the little store said, "You better watch and be careful. The Jordan River is swift and dangerous and deep at this point." We waded out about four feet from the bank. The water was up to his arms, and we baptized the young man. I've never seen anything quite like it. All the way back to Jerusalem, about 12 miles (you know from Jericho to Jerusalem is two days up and one day back — it is every bit up or down hill), this young Armenian man sang: "Oh Happy Day," "What a Friend We Have in Jesus," "Amazing Grace," and many other of those wonderful old-time songs.

I tell you this because there are some who say that John the Baptist couldn't have immersed because there is not enough water in the Jordan River to immerse. That just isn't so. There is enough water in the Jordan River to immerse many, many, many times over. The meaning of the word baptize is to dip, plunge, submerge or cover up. John 1:31 says, "And I knew him not: but that he should be made manifest to Israel, therefore am I come baptizing with water."

John's baptism lasted until Pentecost. After the church was established on the first Pentecost following the resurrection of Jesus, anybody who was baptized with the baptism of John the Baptist had to be baptized again. In Acts 19, Paul found some people at Ephesus who had been immersed with the baptism of John the Baptist; that is a baptism of repentance unto remission of sins looking forward to the coming of the Messiah. Paul said in essence, "This won't do now. You have to be baptized right." So the Bible says he took 12 of them and re-baptized them. It is true that we don't have to be baptized but one time, but we want to be sure we have the right baptism that one time, baptism into Jesus.

Second, I want to talk for a moment about the Holy Spirit baptism. John the Baptist promised that Christ would baptize with the Holy Spirit in Matthew 3:11. The same promise was repeated by Christ to His apostles in Acts 1:5. They were also told to wait in Jerusalem for the power on high. The Lord didn't leave the establishment of the church to a group of uneducated fishermen relying on their own wisdom. They were men who were baptized with the Holy Spirit.

This promise of Holy Spirit baptism was fulfilled on Pentecost when the church was established. The apostles were overwhelmed with the Holy Spirit. Every man heard in the language wherein he was born. Holy Spirit baptism was a promise that Christ made to His apostles; it was never a command. No one has ever in the Bible been commanded to be baptized with Holy Spirit baptism. The Holy Spirit's purpose was, according to John 14:26, to "teach you [the apostles] all things, and bring all things to your remembrance, whatsoever I have said unto you." Jesus simply didn't leave the writing of His new will, the New Testament, to a group of unlearned men. He said the Holy Spirit would come to teach and guide them. They were going to be baptized in the Holy Spirit who was going to bring to their memory all things that He had taught them. It enabled the apostles to perform various miracles, to confirm the Word of God, to prove that the Bible was the Word of God.

For some of us reared in bigotry and prejudice, it is also hard to understand that God is no respecter of persons.

Now there is one other case of Holy Spirit baptism in the Bible. There are just two. One is in Acts 2 on the apostles on Pentecost, and the other was like a gift poured out on the Gentiles in Acts 11:17. It is hard for us to understand the prejudice the Jews had against the Gentiles. Even these Jewish Christians in Acts 11 could not understand that God is no respecter of persons. For some of us reared in bigotry and prejudice, it is also hard to understand that God is no respecter of persons. One of the bright things in the church today is that we are beginning to understand this great principle. It seems so hard for human beings to really grasp it. Here the very apostles of Jesus just couldn't understand that the Gentiles were to have the Gospel on the same terms as the Jews. They didn't understand that we are one in Christ. To convince them, we find the baptism of the Holy Spirit at the first conversion of Gentiles, Cornelius and his household. This was to convince both Jews and Gentiles that the blessings of salvation are for all races of men on the same terms. We are one in Christ Jesus. This is made clear in Acts 15:8-9 and Acts 10:44-48.

These are the only cases of Holy Spirit baptism mentioned in the Bible. Those who claim the baptism of the Holy Spirit today are honest, good, sincere people, but they have been misled. They cannot remember all that Jesus taught; they cannot raise the dead; they cannot drink deadly poison and live. They are good, honest, sincere people in doctrinal error.

I believe the Bible. I believe it to be the sole guide in matters of religion.

Third, I want to talk about the baptism of the Great Commission. After Jesus arose from the grave, He commanded the apostles, "Go ye therefore, and teach all nations, baptizing them in the name of the Father, and of the Son, and of the Holy Ghost" (Matthew 28:19). This was a command and was to be a command as long as the age shall last, until the end of the world. It was water baptism. I know it was water baptism because we read of an example of it in Acts 8:36-39.

I met with a group in Baton Rouge, Louisiana, one time. They said, "We want you to come and tell us what you believe." I went, and I said, "I believe the Bible. I believe it to be the sole guide in matters of religion. Therefore, I believe in the deity of Christ; the brotherhood of man; the fatherhood of God; the church of our Lord; the plan of salvation." One lady raised her hand and said, "I want to know where in the Bible it says anything about being baptized with water. I've never read it." I said, "Well, it is obvious, my dear, that you have never read the Bible. Open your Bible to the eighth chapter of the book of Acts and start reading with verse 36." As we read I put the emphasis on "water": "They came unto a certain *water*: and the eunuch said, See, here is *water*; what doth hinder me to be baptized? And Philip said, If thou believest with all thine heart, thou mayest. And he answered and said, I believe that Jesus Christ is the Son of God. And he commanded the chariot to stand still: and they went down both into the *water*, both Philip and the eunuch; and he baptized him. And when they were come up out of the *water*, the Spirit of the Lord caught away Philip." I believe if she had had false teeth, they would have fallen out. "Well, I declare! Yes, it is really there."

The baptism of the Great Commission is to last until the end of time — in the name of the Father, the Son and the Holy Spirit — immersion in water for the remission of sins. It is the "one baptism" referred to in Ephesians 4:5. It is to last for all time, and its purpose is for the penitent believer, that his sins may be forgiven and washed away. It puts him into Christ, and it enters him into a new life. It was Peter who said, "Repent, and be baptized every one of you in the name of Jesus Christ for the remission of sins" (Acts 2:38) It was Ananias who said to Saul of Tarsus in Acts 22:16, "Now why tarriest thou?

arise, and be baptized, and wash away thy sins, calling on the name of the Lord."

It is in Galatians 3:27 that we are told we are baptized into — i-n-t-o — into Christ. We know what that means. We came into this building. You can't come into it when you are already in it, and you can't be baptized into Christ if you are already in Christ. Faith, repentance, confession and the actual obedience — the obedience of that form of doctrine — puts us into Christ. Romans 6:4 also explains it.

Let me say a word for our dear, sweet, young people. I want you to be on your toes and be wary when you hear something new about one or two or three of these areas. It seems that some of the brethren just cannot stay with the old paths and the ancient landmarks. They have to find something new that Brother Hardeman, Brother Boles, Brother Lipscomb and all our preachers just never found in the Bible in a lifetime of study.

Here are some things that we need to look out for. One is the Lord's Supper. Of all things that we ought to have hobbies about it, ought not to be the Lord's Supper. There are those who think everybody ought to drink out of the same cup. I knew a church in Mississippi that thought everybody had to drink out of the same cup. Then they split the church because some of them said it wasn't a cup — it was a glass. Well, the cup, the container for the fruit of the vine, represents exactly the same thing as the plate represents — absolutely nothing. What does the plate represent? Nothing. It is the container for the bread. It is the bread that represents. What does the container for the fruit of the vine represent? Exactly what the container for the bread represents, nothing.

Others get off on the hobby that the fruit of the vine has to be fermented. I said to some brethren, "Does this fruit of the vine have to be fermented?" "'Oh, yes," they replied. "It has been this way for years." The war came along, and they couldn't get red wine. All they could get was white wine. Some of our brethren went in the liquor store for white wine. One elder said, "I'll admit it tastes like whiskey that I drank as a young man." I said, "Can't we go to the fruit of the vine; can't we go to grape juice? It represents everything in Scripture. Don't you think the juice is the best?" Today that congregation serves the fruit of the vine, but I wasn't going to split the church over it. As long as you have the fruit of the vine, you are with the Bible.

Another hobby is about the Holy Spirit. For years people have been off on the Holy Spirit, claiming to speak in tongues and work miracles. The Holy Spirit works through the Word of God. Don't you forget it.

Another area, nowadays in particular, is marriage and divorce. It is hard for a preacher to accept what the Bible says about marriage and divorce, particularly if he has a son or a daughter or a dear loved one who hasn't followed the Bible's teaching. The Bible hasn't changed. It still teaches the dignity and sanctity of Christian marriage.

Another area is grace. Some of our brethren are off on grace, not quite to the old denominational doctrine of "faith only," but almost.

Recently in the church, we have some people who are off on baptism. We have had some teaching that baptism is a miracle. There is just one thing wrong with that. When I heard that, I wondered if Brother Hardeman, Brother Lipscomb, Brother Baxter and these great men under whom I have studied did not know that. There is just one thing wrong with the teaching that baptism is a miracle: It just ain't so.

A miracle is the setting aside of the natural law in an unexplainable event. It is true that the creation of Adam was a miracle. But, brothers, all the births from Adam are born by natural law — with the one exception of the virgin birth of our Blessed Lord. Now, to say that the birth of a baby is marvelous, yes; complex, yes; wonderful, yes; glorious, yes; precious, yes. But to say it is a miracle just isn't so. To say that baptism is a miracle just isn't right. It is not the setting aside of natural law. It is explained in crystal clear language where a third-grader can understand it in Romans 6:3-4: "Know ye not, that so many of us as were baptized into Jesus Christ were baptized into his death? Therefore we are buried with him by baptism into death: that like as Christ was raised up from the dead by the glory of the Father, even so we also should walk in newness of life." Wonderful, yes; glorious, yes; precious, yes; amazing, yes; a miracle, no.

I want to urge our boys and girls to be on your toes when you hear strange doctrines. People haven't found something new in the Bible. They are just leaving the old paths and the ancient landmarks. You stay with the Book and stay with the Truth.

The fourth baptism is the baptism of suffering. The Bible says in Luke 12:50, "I have a baptism to be baptized with; and how am I straitened till it be accomplished!" Jesus is talking about the baptism of suffering. One has only to enter the Garden of Gethsemane and follow our blessed Lord to the cross to see how overwhelmed, submerged in grief, and in suffering He was. In a way, the Garden of Gethsemane is almost sadder than the Cross. It is true that on the cross, His body was crucified. But in the garden His soul was crucified. "Father, if thou be willing, remove this cup from me: nevertheless not my will, but thine, be done" (Luke 22:42). It was for me that Jesus died on the Cross of Calvary, and it was for me He went through that baptism of suffering.

I want to urge our boys and girls to be on your toes when you hear strange doctrines. People haven't found something new in the Bible. They are just leaving the old paths and the ancient landmarks.

Last is the baptism of fire. John the Baptist mentions it in our Matthew 3 text. Some of the people John was teaching would not repent and would someday experience the fires of torment. Verse 12 clearly shows what John had in mind when he spoke of the baptism of fire: They will be divided in that last day and some will be burned with unquenchable fire. Matthew 5:22 says that if we call our brother a fool, we are in danger of hell fire. James 3:6 speaks of it. At the very end of the Bible, in Revelation 20, we are told about this baptism of fire. I pray we will never experience it. "And the sea gave up the dead which were in it; and death and hell delivered up the dead which were in them: and they were judged every man according to their works. And death and hell were cast into the lake of fire. This is the second death. And whosoever was not found written in the book of life was cast into the lake of fire."

I'm glad my name is on that church roll we keep in our records office. I'm glad it is there, but that is not the important thing. I'm glad that many years ago I was baptized into Christ with the Great Commission baptism down in Shoal Creek. I don't know whether they put my name on it or if we had a record book at Ethridge Church of Christ. But that day my name was enrolled in the Lamb's Book of Life. That is what is going to count in that last day.

Dearly beloved, if there is one in this church audience this morning who has never obeyed that one baptism of Ephesians 4:5: "One Lord, one faith, one baptism," I want you to obey it today. Would you come, believing in Jesus, turning from sin, being baptized into Christ today so your name will be enrolled in the Lamb's Book of Life?

∾

Madison Church of Christ
Madison, Tennessee
September 14, 1980, a.m.

The Holy Spirit

I appreciate a recent letter from a lovely young lady who asked several questions about the Holy Spirit. I think really she is asking five questions. I want to discuss them today. I do not, as you know, discuss a doctrinal issue every Lord's Day. I think we must have preaching and teaching on doctrinal issues and we must have a lot of preaching and teaching on Christian living. But today I want to talk about doctrine as it relates to the Holy Spirit.

First, what is the Holy Spirit? A better question would be *who* is the Holy Spirit? It would be like asking, "What is the Christ?" That is not quite correct. We should say, "Who is the Christ? Who is the Holy Spirit?" The answer is the Holy Spirit is an entity, a personality. The Holy Spirit is never referred to in the Scriptures as "it." The Scriptures always say "He." God is a personality, an entity. Christ is also a personality, a being, an entity. So the

Holy Spirit is a personality, an entity. I don't want to in any way oversimplify this.

Someone says, "Well, aren't the three all one?" Yes, the doctrine of the Trinity is a viable doctrine: God the Father, Christ the Son, and the Holy Spirit the Comforter. There are three distinct personalities and three distinct entities, yet in purpose and in plan they are one.

So, when do you receive the Holy Spirit? The answer is when you are baptized into Christ.

I think it is similar to what the Bible teaches about the relationship between husband and wife. It is a great mystery. It is a profound truth. It is one that has baffled the scholars through the years. How can you be two and be one? The Bible says about husband and wife, "and they twain shall be one flesh" (Matthew 19:5). Now there are two in the sense that there are two distinct souls, two distinct persons, two distinct beings. Yet so close and profound and marvelous is marriage — that union of two for better or worse, in sickness and in health, till death do us part, so help me God — there are "two hearts that beat as one." One in person, one in plan, one in love, and one in loyalty. It is wonderful! A man is to love his wife even as he loves his own body. So it is with the Holy Spirit. He is a person. He is also part of the Godhead: God the Father, Christ the Son, and the Holy Spirit the Comforter.

Second, she is asking, "How do you get it?" A better question would be, when do you receive the Holy

Spirit? There is so much misunderstanding about the Holy Spirit.

When I was a boy, there was a very fine group of Holiness people who would hold a revival and would preach that we need to get the Holy Spirit. The apostles never taught any such thing as that. We used to go to the Holiness revivals, and, God forgive us, we went for the wrong purpose. We went for the show. The women would come to the mourner's bench and pray for the Holy Spirit. When one of them would get it, there was more shaking and jumping than some of the shows at the county fair. Hollering and rolling, sometimes they even got down on all fours.

Back in the pioneer days it was customary that when people came to the mourner's bench, to pray for the Holy Spirit, all of a sudden they got it; they would take the "barks," and they would get down on all fours — intelligent women, beautifully dressed — and go around the campground on all fours barking like a dog. Or they would take the "jerks." Peter Cartwright said that he has seen their hair come undone (they put their hair in a ball on top of their head in those days), and they would whip their heads with such fervor that the hair would pop like a whip.

Now that's the kind of concept of what it means to receive the Holy Spirit that has held over through the years. Some members of the church of Christ have gone off on that kind of tangent. It is tragic and it is sad. The truth of it is that the Holy Spirit, God the Father, and Christ the Son call us to sanity, to the greatest thing the world has ever known, to the religion of Jesus.

So, when do you receive the Holy Spirit? The answer is when you are baptized into Christ. "Repent, and be baptized every one of you in the name of Jesus Christ for the remission of sins, and ye shall receive the gift of the Holy Ghost" (Acts 2:38). The original Greek conception makes it clear that the gift that you receive is the Holy Spirit. If I tell you to do something and I give you a gift of $100, what is the gift of $100? It is $100. When you hear the Good News of Jesus Christ, believe it, confess Christ, and are baptized, you have God the Father, Christ the Son, and the Holy Spirit the Comforter. You have everything and you are all-in-all. God has withheld nothing from you. The Holy Spirit dwells in your heart. Christ dwells in your heart. God dwells in your heart.

Third, how does the Holy Spirit operate? The Bible teaches us that the Holy Spirit teaches and witnesses (Acts 5:32; John 15:26). The Holy Spirit speaks; the Holy Spirit comforts; the Holy Spirit advises. He points; He knows; He can be resisted; He can be blasphemed. I could take time to give you book, chapter and verse for all those things, but you know they are there.

So how does He do all these things? How does the Holy Spirit operate? There are two explanations: One is in error, and one is true. The one in error is the Holy Spirit operates directly in your heart, talks to you, tells you what to do directly. And only God knows the sins that have been covered up by this kind of theory. Occasionally, I hear of a preacher who leaves his wife, goes off after another woman, and explains that the Holy Spirit has guided him and told him to do it. I asked once, "Did you keep that preacher after he went off with this other woman?" The answer was, "Oh yeah, we kept him." I asked, "Why?" They said, "The Holy Spirit told him to do it."

I cannot accept, from a lifetime of Bible study, that God the Father, Christ the Son, or the Holy Spirit the Comforter would lead you or guide you in any way, shape, form or fashion that is contrary to the Word of God.

Reminds me of a deacon in Nashville a couple of years ago who was asked, "How is the church getting along where you go?" He said, "We have had a little problem. We had $10,000 in the treasury, and the preacher embezzled it. The rascal ran off with it." The fellow said, "That's bad." The deacon said, "That's not too awfully bad. We caught him down in New Orleans." The man said, "Are you going to prosecute him?" He said, "No we are bringing him back to Nashville and make him preach it out." I take the same view of that as I would take if a preacher robbed the Third National Bank and when he was caught, he said, "I've been praying over this now, prayed over it, prayed over it and prayed over it — and the Holy Spirit told me to rob this bank." If I were the judge, I'd say, "Son, I have a little contact with the Holy Spirit and the Holy Spirit says to me, 'Thou shalt not steal.' You are going to have go to the penitentiary for about 20 years, and maybe you will kinda' learn how the Holy Spirit operates."

I could take up all my time telling you more stories like that. I'm not saying those people are not honest. I'm not saying they are not sincere. I'm not saying if a man wants to sin, if he will pray over it long enough and wants it badly enough and believes that the Holy Spirit speaks to him directly, he won't get the signal. But what I am saying is that the Holy Spirit operates through His instrument: the Word of God: "And take ... the sword of the Spirit, which is the word of God" (Ephesians 6:17). I cannot accept, from a lifetime of Bible study, that God the Father, Christ the Son or the Holy Spirit the Comforter would lead you or guide you in any way, shape, form or fashion that is contrary to the Word of God.

Someone says, "Do you mean to say that the Holy Spirit is just the Bible?" Of course not. I don't believe this is God that I hold in my hand, but I believe with all of my heart it is the Word of God. I do not believe for one minute that this is Christ, the Son of God, that I hold in my hand, but I believe with all of my heart that it is the revelation of Jesus Christ. And without what I hold in my hand, what would you know about Jesus? Only what Josephus and a few historians say, which is very skimpy and very little. No, I do not believe that this Bible I hold in my hand is the Holy Spirit any more than I believe it is God the Father or Christ the Son. I believe it is the Word of God, and I believe Christ Jesus is made known through what I hold in my hand. I believe with all of my heart that the Holy Spirit inspired this Word of God. And if you want to know what the Holy Spirit would have you do, if you want to know where the Holy Spirit would guide you, then here it is. This is the sword of the Spirit, which is the Word of God — alive and sharp and powerful and glorious and wonderful. The Bible won't put you in the sawdust. It will cause you to walk straight, and it will call you to sanity.

Fourth, what is the speaking in tongues? The speaking in tongues in the Bible is the speaking in a language. If you will read Acts 2 before you get to the Corinthian letter, you will understand that every man heard in the tongue wherein he was born. When the church was established in Acts 2, men were gathered together from every nation. If you go to the United Nations, you can understand the tremendous problem you can have with lots of languages. There are many countries where you only have to go a few miles and you find a completely different language. Did you know all the churches of Asia were within about 50 miles of each other? You know that even in that part of the world today, and in some other parts of the world, you can go down the street and hear a dozen languages spoken. It is hard for us in America to understand that. We have 50 states. If we had 50 languages and if these good people from Colorado Springs spoke another language, they would have extreme difficulty understanding what I was saying. Same would be true if those from Maryland spoke another language and those from Alabama another.

Now the gift of languages was one of the spiritual gifts given to the early church before the New Testament was written. When those early Christians crossed a border, they didn't have to spend 50 years studying the language to become proficient in it. The great miracle of languages brought in the church. The gift of languages flourished. I believe with all of my heart that when that which was perfect was come and the New Testament was complete, the spiritual gifts that were given temporarily to the early church ceased.

Now the people who believe the Holy Spirit is mystic, better felt than told, will not accept that. So there has come the emotional phenomenon of the unknown jabber. I could understand it, and I could interpret it if I wanted to. If Brother Ruhl would get up here and rattle off like a man who had lost his senses, I'd stand right here and make up an interpretation. How would he know because he doesn't know what he is saying? He is making up the unknown jabber. You put a Greek New Testament in front of the folks who claim to speak in tongues and they wouldn't know alpha from omega. You put a Hebrew New Testament in front of them, and they wouldn't even know the language was written backwards.

The world needs Jesus so badly. The poor need to be fed. The homeless need a father and a mother. There is so much to be done, and here are religious people babbling on in a silly, ridiculous jabber like a baby. Don't tell me that is the religion of Jesus. There isn't anything to substantiate it in the whole Bible. Things were done decently and in order. The speaking in tongues was a gift of languages in the early church, present until the New Testament was completed.

Fifth, what is the blasphemy against the Holy Spirit, and why can it not be forgiven? The Bible says everything will be forgiven except the blasphemy of the Holy Spirit (Matthew 12:31). A lot of people are very concerned about whether or not they can be forgiven. The word "blaspheme" means to set aside. I want to give you what I believe to be the clearest, the most logical, the safest, the soundest explanation I have heard of the sin against the Holy Spirit.

Sometimes I have someone come to me who has committed adultery and say, "I just know I can never be forgiven. I know this is the sin against the Holy Spirit." I say, "You couldn't be worse wrong. Jesus said to the woman taken in adultery, 'Go, and sin no more' (John 8:11). That is what I say today to you. If you haven't been baptized into Christ, you come and be baptized into Christ, and everything you have ever done wrong will be washed away in the blood. If you have been baptized, renew your heart and dedicate your own heart, clean up your life and live right."

If you set aside the teaching of the Holy Spirit through the Word of God, there will be no forgiveness here or hereafter.

When John the Baptist came, many rejected him. But those who rejected John had another opportunity, for Christ our Lord followed John. But there were those who were going to reject Jesus' personal ministry. Yet, even they had another chance when the church was established. I'm convinced that of the 3,000 baptized on the Day of Pentecost, there had been many who had refused John and rejected Jesus. Jesus says, "When I am gone, the Holy Spirit is coming." The Holy Spirit did come and guided the apostles in all the truth. But if you set aside the teaching of the Holy Spirit through the Word of God, there will be no forgiveness here or hereafter. Those who rejected John, had an opportunity to hear and to receive Jesus. Those who rejected both John and Jesus had another chance to hear the Word of God inspired by the Holy Spirit. But for those who reject the New Testament, there won't be anything left.

A setting aside of the new will of Jesus, a complete and final rejection of the New Testament, will not be forgiven in this world or in the world to come. There won't be another John the Baptist, another Jesus or another New Testament. As long as you can believe in Jesus Christ, as long as you can be sorry for the mistakes you have made and be determined to turn from them, as long as you can confess the sweet name of Jesus, as long as you can be baptized into Christ, whatever you have done wrong can be forgiven forever. Even after you have done that, if you wander away, you can be forgiven as long as you are willing to come back like the prodigal and say, "I'm sorry. I want forgiveness. I want to live right." You can be forgiven.

I'm sorry about the controversy over the Holy Spirit in some areas of our country, but it has been that way for hundreds of years. When I was a boy, people were arguing over the Holy Spirit. The answers I bring you today are scriptural, biblical, sane and sound. As long as you live by the teaching of this Book; giving your heart and soul to Christ Jesus; loving your neighbor as yourself; loving God with all of your heart; being faithful and true to the church of our Lord and to Christ, you can rest assured that God is yours, Christ is yours, the Holy Spirit is yours. They shall dwell with you, and heaven shall be your home.

I want to say a word to our young people. You don't know how proud I am of you, that you haven't been carried away with some of this modern emotionalism. A little group of people huddled over here talking in a unknown jabber when there is a lost and dying world that needs to know about Jesus, when there are hundreds of little children who need a papa and a mama and love and care, when there are people who are poor and lowly and downtrodden who need hope. Let us be out in the real world where the babies are being born and the people are dying, telling them about Jesus and His love, inviting them to know this Christ of the Bible and God, and the Holy Spirit shall be theirs.

Will you come today?

❧

Madison Church of Christ
Madison, Tennessee
November 19, 1972, a.m.

The Resurrection

Ladies and gentlemen, it seems to me that it is so easy to believe in a resurrection when you live in Middle Tennessee. Of all the places I have ever seen on this planet, none other is so soul stirring, heartwarming or thrilling in its beauty as our native Middle Tennessee. How easy to believe in a resurrection when you want to believe and when you live in beautiful Middle Tennessee.

Brother Robert Kerse, who preaches at Penington Bend, and I were fishing on Dale Hollow Lake this past week. I didn't get a bite all day, but we enjoyed it. Brother Kerse said, "Ira, wasn't God Almighty at His best when He made our Middle Tennessee?" I said, "There is no doubt about that."

We see God's handiwork in nature. God puts it to sleep in the winter time when everything goes brown and dull, the snows and the rains come, and all is dead. Then one day it bursts forth into glorious green; flowers bloom; the birds sing. It is resurrection time in beautiful, lovely Middle Tennessee. It is so easy to believe.

All of 1 Corinthians 15 deals with the Resurrection, and the passage is rather lengthy. I want to share it with you today. There were some people at Corinth who were teaching that there is not going to be a resurrection. God is dead; He is gone; there will never be a resurrection. So Paul gives this learned treatise to counteract that false doctrine.

He begins by saying: "Moreover, brethren, I declare unto you the gospel which I preached unto you, which also ye have received, and wherein ye stand; by which also ye are saved, if ye keep in memory what I preached unto you, unless ye have believed in vain. For I delivered unto you first of all that which I also received, how that Christ died for our sins according to the scriptures; And that he was buried, and that he rose again the third day according to the scriptures: And that he was seen of Cephas, then of the twelve: After that, he was seen of above five hundred brethren at once; of whom the greater part remain unto this present, but some are fallen asleep."

Now the death, burial and resurrection of our Lord occurred about A.D. 30. Paul wrote this epistle we are studying about A.D. 57, 27 years after the Resurrection. No wonder he said that many of these who saw the Lord and are witnesses are still alive to this day.

I want you to think a minute: Can you remember 27 years ago? A lot of you can't. You were not born then. I remember 27 years ago. I graduated from

Abilene Christian that spring. I went to Chanute
field and preached to soldiers that fall and went to
the University of Illinois. Our country was engaged
in World War II, in a fight for its very existence.
The nation was united in that great struggle, in
that dreadful year of 1943 — just 27 years ago. I
remember the events of that year as clear as if it
were yesterday.

I want you to raise your hand if you remember 27
years ago. There are several hundred of us here. I'm
a little bit surprised that so many of the women folk
would admit they were just little girls. You know,
you remember a lot when you are a little girl. So it is
very reasonable that Paul says here, in pointing out
all this evidence, that some had fallen asleep but
many of them were living until that good day.

Then he goes on to say, "After that, he was seen of
James; then of all the apostles. And last of all he
was seen of me also, as of one born out of due time.
For I am the least of the apostles, that am not meet
to be called an apostle, because I persecuted the
church of God. But by the grace of God, I am what I
am: and his grace which was bestowed upon me
was not in vain; but I laboured more abundantly
than they all: yet not I, but the grace of God which
was with me."

There are two things I want to share with you
from this passage. Sometimes we have deep feelings
of guilt because we have done some terrible things.
I've counseled with many a Christian, and I convinced that God had forgiven them, their family had
forgiven them, their neighbors and friends had forgiven them, but they had an unbelievable burden of

guilt on their hearts. The reason was they were not willing to forgive themselves. This ought to be an inspiration to us. Jesus said that he who is forgiven much, loves much (Luke 7:47). The fact that you have done some terrible, awful thing in the past — as Paul had done when he murdered Christians — it should just make you appreciate Christ and His grace and mercy and forgiveness and rejoice in Him even more.

Whenever I read this verse I think of our Brother Brewer who was answering questions at a meeting. In the olden days during a revival meeting, a question box was set up. Anybody who wanted to ask a question put it in the box. Then the preacher would answer it that night. That was an attraction. People looked forward to it.

Brother Otis Gatewood was out in Utah one time and they turned in this question: "Is Job's turkey dead yet?" He read the question and said, "From the looks of this scratching, he is still alive. Next question."

I think the man that was the best at knowing how to answer was Marshall Keeble. He was in Atlanta, Georgia, and had baptized dozens. The question was turned in: "Who was Cain's wife?" Brother Keeble put his glasses down on his nose, read the question, and shouted out at the top of his voice: "Mrs. Cain."

Sometimes the questions got a little personal. One time when Brother Brewer was holding a meeting, this question was put in the box: "What on earth makes you so mortal ugly?" Brother Brewer turned to the passage we are reading today (1 Corinthians 15:10) and replied, "By the grace of God, I am what I am." A deep answer to a silly question.

Paul relied on the grace of God instead of his own goodness, and when you do that, you can forgive yourself, even for murder, or killing Christians, or destroying the church. "Therefore whether it were I or they, so we preach, and so ye believed."

The Resurrection is the heart of the Christian religion and the basis of our hope.

Next in this resurrection chapter, Paul points out that Christ's resurrection proves that there will be a resurrection for us all. "Now if Christ be preached that he rose from the dead, how say some among you that there is no resurrection of the dead? But if there be no resurrection of the dead, then is Christ not risen: And if Christ be not risen, then is our preaching vain, and your faith is also vain. Yea, and we are found false witnesses of God; because we have testified of God that he raised up Christ: whom he raised not up, if so be that the dead rise not. For if the dead rise not, then is not Christ raised: And if Christ be not raised, your faith is vain: ye are yet in your sins. Then they also which are fallen asleep in Christ are perished. If in this life only we have hope in Christ, we are of all men most miserable."

Brethren, the Resurrection is the heart of the Gospel of Christ. If there is no resurrection, have Paul and these apostles lied and made up all this story about Jesus Christ? If so, Paul said our hope is in vain; we are still in our sins; and we are the most pitiful people in the world because we have given up everything — prestige, power, good job, good name

— for Christ Jesus. We've been beaten, stoned and shipwrecked. Paul says, "Now does that make sense for intelligent men to do all that as a hoax, for something they just made up?" Then he said, "If Christ is not raised, it is all in vain." Yes, the Resurrection is the heart of the Christian religion and the basis of our hope.

Then Paul testified in the next few verses that Christ will reign until all enemies are put under His feet. The last enemy to be conquered will be death. "But now is Christ risen from the dead, and become the firstfruits of them that slept. For since by man came death, by man came also the resurrection of the dead." He's talking about Adam, who sinned and brought death into the world, and Christ, who brought life.

Verse 22: "For as in Adam all die, even so in Christ shall all be made alive. But every man in his own order: Christ the firstfruits; afterward they that are Christ's at his coming. Then cometh the end, when he shall have delivered up the kingdom to God, even the Father; when he shall have put down all rule and all authority and power. For he must reign, till he hath put all enemies under his feet. The last enemy that shall be destroyed is death." When Christ comes, the resurrection will happen — when the people are raised from the dead and those who are alive are changed in a moment, in a twinkling of an eye. Christ will present us to God, and that will be the end of death.

Here He gives the kingdom back; you remember He told His disciples: "All power [authority] is given unto me in heaven and in earth" (Matthew 28:18).

When the world comes to an end — when the resurrection comes; when the judgment day comes; when the Lord Jesus presents all of His people to God — then all enemies are conquered and all things returned to God that they may be all in all. "And when all things shall be subdued unto him, then shall the Son also himself be subject unto him that put all things under him, that God may be all in all" (1 Corinthians 15:28).

Now comes what is considered to be one of the most difficult passages in all the Bible. I think we have made it harder than it really is. Verse 29: "Else what shall they do which are baptized for the dead, if the dead rise not at all? why are they then baptized for the dead?"

We have tried to explain this verse every way in the world. I think the best explanation is to just accept what he says. There were some in the church at Corinth teaching there would be no resurrection, and yet there were some who were baptizing the living for somebody who had already died. Paul didn't condone it. He didn't say "we." He didn't say the church in general. He said "they."

There is a name for this kind of logic by logicians. It was used by Jesus when the people said to Him, "Oh yes, You open the eyes of the blind; You cause the lame to walk; and You are doing all these things, but You are doing them by the power of the devil; by the power of Beelzebub." Jesus just took them at their own word and said, "All right, if I by Beelzebub cast out Beelzebub — if the devil cast out the devil how is the devil going to stand? For a house divided against itself cannot stand" (Matthew 12:22-27).

These people who didn't believe in the resurrection, some of them, were baptizing for the dead.

Remember this: If you are not ready to meet God when the breath leaves your body, there is not a second that your soul will have peace.

Paul didn't endorse it; we know that it is not taught in the Scriptures. The Bible says that every man must give an account of himself (Romans 14:12). There are some things a man has to do for himself. If I could, I would be baptized for any unbaptized person in this building — but I can't. I have talked to precious old Christian mothers with tears rolling down their cheeks when they tell me about some son they love better than anything in the world, but he would not come to Christ. Don't you know that mother would be baptized for that boy if she could? Of course, she would. Don't you know that daughter would be baptized for her old dad if she could?

I never will forget holding a meeting one time and a nephew of a U. S. Senator from Indiana was there. He was a young fellow about 28 years old, handsome and strong, married to this pretty woman about the same age. When we closed that meeting, when we sang that last song, tears stated pouring down her cheeks, and she wept the entire time. I knew what she was thinking because she told me: "Brother North, my husband has never been so close to becoming a Christian. He is almost ready; he is almost persuaded; I pray that this meeting will not close without his being baptized. He may never be this close again." That is exactly what happened. I asked somebody up there if he had ever been baptized, and the person said, "No he hasn't, and he has never been as close to it as he was in that meeting some 20 years ago." Don't you think that young wife would have given the world if she could have stepped out that night and been baptized for him? But she couldn't do it.

The point of it is this: These false teachers were teaching there would be no resurrection, yet some of them were baptizing for people who had already died. What were they doing that for, if they didn't think there would be a hereafter, and a God, and a judgment, and a resurrection?

And then Paul says in verse 30: "And why stand we in jeopardy every hour?" Paul says if there is no resurrection and if we didn't see Jesus Christ after the resurrection, then why are we standing in jeopardy? Why are we putting our very lives in danger every day? Do you think we would do that for a lie or a hoax? Verse 31: "I protest by your rejoicing which I have in Christ Jesus our Lord, I die daily. If after the manner of men I have fought with beasts at Ephesus, what advantageth it me, if the dead rise not? let us eat and drink; for to morrow we die." I don't know if Paul actually fought with beasts at Ephesus, or if it was just a symbol of the abusing and the tremendous persecution he faced. But he said, "I'll tell you one thing, we wouldn't be considered the offscouring of the earth and face danger and death every day if the resurrection weren't true; we would "eat, drink and be merry". I think he was right.

I'm not sure that we do the religion of Jesus justice when we say, "Oh, well, there is no hell. But if there is no judgment and there is no hereafter, it is still better to be a Christian." Is it? There might be times when it wouldn't be. For example, take teaching our children to be honest. I don't want young people at Madison to be taught to be honest because it is best; we want to teach them to be honest because it is right. The man who is honest because it is the best policy will, sometime in his life, cheat or lie because it doesn't look like the best choice right at that moment. But I'll tell you one thing: If he is honest because it is right it doesn't make any difference whether it looks best or not. It is a matter of conviction.

And so it is with the resurrection of Christ. We believe it as a matter of conviction. So we believe it even if the persecution is literal. I had a student in my class one time at Lipscomb who said, "Brother North, you people don't know what it is to sacrifice to be a Christian. It is popular over here. When I was baptized over in Germany, I was disinherited. When I left the state church, I was ostracized; I was an outcast. If you were in Europe when you were baptized and were disinherited by your family and considered an outcast from society, then you would understand."

I was in Florence, Italy, a few years ago and saw the most encouraging thing I saw in Europe: a little school for preachers. Brother Gibbs said, "Do you see these 21 boys here preparing to preach the Gospel of Christ? They know what it is to suffer for Christ. Every one of them has been disinherited by their families because they left the Roman church. They can't get a job except as day laborers because when the religious leaders pass the word around, they are considered as traitors. Those boys have conviction." No wonder there is a little church of Christ in every city in Italy. When you have men who believe in the resurrection that strong, when you have men with conviction like that, the job will be done.

You never give a penny, you never give a moment of time; you don't do anything for the Lord that is in vain. It will be there when you cross over the river.

But some in Corinth had answered, "My, if there is a resurrection, where will the body be?" Then Paul uses an analogy we are familiar with. He answered more tersely than we could. He was an inspired man. I would not have put it this strong, but he did and it is all right. "Thou fool, that which thou sowest is not quickened, except it die." And then he says, "Don't you know when you plant a seed in the ground what comes forth? It is different from that seed, but it is just a glorious body from that seed. It is still the same." And he says, "So it shall be in the resurrection what comes forth will be different; it was sown in weakness, it will be raised in might; it was sown in weakness, it will be raised in power; it was sown in dishonor, it will be raised in honor; it was sown corruptible, it will be raised incorruptible." If it was mortal, it will become immortal. But it will be the same. It is true that we do not know all about that resurrected body, but I'll tell you one thing: The Bible says it does not yet appear what we'll be like, but we will be like Him, for we will see Him like He is.

When you are working out in your garden, in the flowers, pick up a handful of dirt sometime and concentrate on it. When you look at that handful of dirt, I want you to think about that lovely woman who is your wife or your sweetheart or your precious mother, someone very near and dear to you. God made the body of that dear one from dirt, and it will go back to that dirt. "For dust thou art, and unto dust shalt thou return" (Genesis 3:19) was spoken about the body. You can embalm it; you can bury it in a copper casket that cost $4,500, you can put it in a tomb that cost a million. But, let's face it, it is going back to dust. Don't you know that God, who from a handful of dirt made anything as wonderful as that wife of yours, don't you think that God can raise you in the last days and give you an immortal body? Of course He can, and we believe it. For it is the heart of our faith and the heart of our hope.

Then in the last verses Paul addresses the argument that many of them were thinking about: what about those of who are alive when Jesus comes? We are not going to be raised from the dead. Paul says, "Behold, I shew you a mystery; We shall not all sleep, but we shall all be changed, In a moment, in the twinkling of an eye, at the last trump: for the trumpet shall sound, and the dead shall be raised incorruptible, and we shall be changed." Paul further says that the dead in Christ will rise first and we that are alive will be caught up together with them in the clouds (1 Thessalonians 4:14-17).

Brother Brewer talked Wednesday night on "Where Are the Dead?" He did a beautiful job and pointed out that if you are ready to meet God when you die, your soul goes to Paradise, a place of rest. Jesus said, "To day shalt thou be with me in paradise" (Luke 23:43). Paul says that when you are absent from the body, you are present with the Lord (2 Corinthians 5). If you are ready to meet God when you die, you go to Paradise to await the resurrection and the judgment. If you are unprepared, you go to Tartarus, a place of unrest for the wicked. Remember this: If you are not ready to meet God when the breath leaves your body, there is not a second that your soul will have peace. Not one second's peace when you die, if you are not ready to meet God. That is why at funerals, we ought to be very careful about saying somebody is better off. That all depends on how they lived. If they are in Paradise, they are better off; if they are in Tartarus, waiting for the judgment and hell, or Gehenna, they are not better off. Paul says that you do err because in that great day they that are alive and don't experience death will experience a translation and a transformation. So you will be changed just like that, when the sea gives up its dead and the grave gives up its dead (Revelation 20:13).

Then he closes in verse 58 by telling them what to do since all this is true: "Therefore, my beloved brethren, be ye stedfast, unmoveable, always abounding in the work of the Lord, forasmuch as ye know that your labour is not in vain in the Lord."

Dearly beloved, the organized church in America is sick this morning. Religion is on the decline, and

I'm going to tell you one reason I believe it is declining: the very fact that we have this Great News of the resurrection. What have we done with it? Built this building, a beautiful parking lot, air conditioning. Millions we have spent on sticks and stones and talking. But what have we done for homeless children? What have we done for the aged? What have we done for the poor? What have we really done as far as action is concerned? Practically nothing. Our inner city today is leaderless, churchless and godless.

I'm going to tell you one thing: By the grace of God Almighty, we on this corner intend to indoctrinate these young people so they will carry on. When the Lord Jesus comes again, if there is a free United States of America, there has got to be a church of Christ on this corner. We ain't going to run, and we are not going to sit down and play dead. We are not going to be known for a lot of talk. We are going to abound in the work of the Lord always.

A young man, with a tremendous education, who works in this part of town, came into my office a few months ago. He said, "I want you to know that when I came here, I came because my wife was putting the pressure on me; I wasn't sure I believed any more. I thought maybe the church didn't belong to our age. It is just talk, talk, talk. But I want to make a confession." I asked, "What are you confessing?" He said, "Number one: I am delighted. I'm happy as I can be. I'm involved in helping little children. Let me tell you another thing: I do believe that Jesus Christ is the Son of God."

I told Dr. Baxter about that conversation, and he said, "You know, Ira, he didn't need a lot of theological argument, did he? He just needed involvement, action."

Stand fast; keep your convictions; and abound in the work of the Lord. Let us have some activity and action. Why? Because your labor is not in vain in the Lord. You never give a penny, you never give a moment of time, you don't do anything for the Lord that is in vain. It will be there when you cross over the river.

The resurrection of Jesus ought not to make us smug and self-righteous, but filled with the grace of God.

Oh, I want us to be known in the years ahead as the church that practices what it preaches, not as a church that holds a mere form of the Lord's Supper with a big fine building or that has a lot of preaching, but one that backs up its talk with what it does — not only with the preaching but with the practice. Not only with the convictions of the action, because you know that conviction will produce action, but action that will produce that conviction.

I was so thrilled this week when I went over to the kitchen where women were cooking for old people who are blind and sick and unable to care for themselves. They said, "Sit down; we will feed you." That was as fine a meal as I ever ate. It was cooked with the love of Jesus. Young women were coming by to get trays and delivering them to old people. It is no wonder the elderly people weep when those dear people knock on their door and say, "We are from the Madison church of Christ. We have brought you a hot meal." No wonder.

I tell you right now: You can't beat that "abounding in the work of the Lord." The resurrection of Jesus ought not to make us smug and self-righteous, but filled with the grace of God, with real conviction backed up with action, knowing that our labor is not in vain for Jesus. Will you come today?

∾

Madison Church of Christ
Madison, Tennessee
March 29, 1970, a.m.

Get Ready for the Judgement

In Matthew 25:31 we have a most significant passage. Here the Lord Jesus pulls back the curtain, as it were, and gives us a glimpse of the judgment day. Now all of us who believe in God, in the deity of Christ, and in the inspiration of the Holy Scriptures believe there will be a judgement day. We believe there will be a day when all the books will be balanced and all accounts settled. The God of heaven shall gather before Him all nations, and man shall give account before his Maker.

I want to read beginning with verse 31 the remaining part of the chapter that tells us of the judgment. I want you to meditate on it, and then we will study it together. "When the Son of man shall come in his glory, and all the holy angels with him, then shall he sit upon the throne of his glory: And before Him shall be gathered all nations: and he shall separate them one from another, as a shepherd divideth his sheep from the goats: And he shall set the sheep on his right hand, but the goats on the left. Then shall the King say unto them on his right hand, Come, ye blessed of my Father, inherit the kingdom prepared for you from the foundation of the world: For I was an hungred, and ye gave me meat: I was thirsty, and ye gave me drink: I was a stranger, and ye took me in: Naked, and ye clothed me: I was sick, and ye visited me: I was in prison, and ye came unto me. Then shall the righteous answer him, saying, Lord, when saw we thee an hungred, and fed thee? or thirsty, and gave thee drink? When saw we thee a stranger, and took thee in? or naked, and clothed thee? Or when saw we thee sick, or in prison, and came unto thee? And the King shall answer and say unto them, Verily I say unto you, Inasmuch as ye have done it unto one of the least of these my brethren, ye have done it unto me. Then shall he say also unto them on the left hand, Depart from me, ye cursed, into everlasting fire, prepared for the devil and his angels: For I was an hungred, and ye gave me no meat: I was thirsty, and ye gave me no drink: I was a stranger, ye took me not in: naked, and ye clothed me not: sick, and in prison, and ye visited me not. Then shall they also answer him, saying, Lord, when saw we thee an hungred or athirst, or a stranger, or naked, or sick, or in prison, and did not minister unto thee? Then shall he answer them, saying, Verily I say unto you, Inasmuch as ye did it not to one of the least of these, ye did it not to me. And these shall go away into everlasting punishment: but the righteous into life eternal."

Dearly beloved, if there is any passage in this Bible we need today, it is this judgment scene. It is so clear

that a child 10 years old with a third-grade education could understand it. Yet, Brother Mid McKnight
says that in churches of Christ today, and I think he
is right, we spend more money and more time on cat
food than we do on helping all these people who
Jesus was talking about. If you don't believe it, get
the bulletin of the average congregation, and just see
what they are doing for the stranger, those in prison,
the poor and the lowly, and the downtrodden.

*The Madison church, as far as I
know, has the largest, most dynamic
benevolent program on earth ...
but we aren't doing half what we
could do.*

Dearly beloved, I'm not fussing on the Madison
church today, but I want to tell you this: It is true
that the Madison church, as far as I know, has the
largest, most dynamic benevolent program on earth
today among churches of Christ. We visit more people in prison and take care of more homeless and
spend more money per week than any church of
Christ in the world, but we aren't doing half what
we could do. We aren't doing half of what we ought
to do, and I don't believe half of what we will do in
the next few years. Oh, this a frightening thing.

I want to share with you the entire 25th chapter
for a moment. You know God Almighty didn't cut the
Bible up into chapters. God Almighty didn't cut the
Bible up in verses. Man did that hundreds of years
after the Bible was written. Sometimes when we
study the Bible, we don't get the context; we don't

get the setting; we don't study it all together. So I want us to take the entire chapter.

What happens first is Jesus tells the powerful parable of the virgins. Five were wise, and five were foolish. They went out to meet the bridegroom, and five of them ran out of oil. They turned to the other five and asked for some of their oil. These five said, "No, we just barely have enough for ourselves. You will have to go and get your own." While they were gone, the bridegroom came and those with oil in their lamps went in and enjoyed the wedding.

Now in New Testament times, when people had a wedding they had a wedding. They made something of it. I like that. I thank God we have a beautiful chapel and a wonderful annex for our young people to get married and have a reception right here. I'll tell you one thing: That is money well spent. Let them get married here at home. Let their wedding be something sweet and precious in their memory all the days of their life. Then when the boat begins to rock, when the going gets rough, they can think back about their wedding and know they are loved by the people here and that we want them to have a strong marriage.

What was Jesus teaching? Was it not this: That we can do good works only for ourselves. Those who had the oil couldn't share with those who had none. They had to have their own. At the judgment bar of God, I'm not going to be able to turn to Brother Roark and say, "I have a big account in the bank of heaven. I want to give you part of mine." The Bible says, "So then, every one of us shall give account of himself to God" (Romans 14:12). Jesus was teaching His disciples: You've got to lay up good works in heaven now because when the Bridegroom cometh — when the trumpet sounds, when the sea and the grave give up their dead, before this old earth dissolves in fervent heat, when Jesus appears to claim His bride, the church — it will be too late. It will be too late to take in a stranger; it will be too late to clothe the naked; it will be too late to take an interest in the poor and the downtrodden; it will be too late to provide for homeless children or neglected children; it will be too late to visit those in prison.

Jesus' next parable is the parable of the talents. Jesus said that a man called his servants in and he gave one five talents; another two; another one. When he came back, the master said to the one who had five, "What have you done?" "I have used the opportunity I had. Here are five more." "Well done, good and faithful servant. You have been faithful over few things. I'll make you ruler over many. Enter thou into the joys of thy Lord." To the man with two talents (moderate opportunity), he said, "What have you done?" "Well, I have used them, and I have two more." "Well done, good and faithful servant. Enter thou into the joys of thy Lord." To the man with just one talent (a little opportunity), he said, "What have you done?" The man said back (in the vernacular), "I ain't done nothing. I was afraid and I hid it and I didn't use my opportunities." "Bind him hand and foot and cast him into outer darkness. There shall be weeping and gnashing of teeth. He is wicked, and he is slothful."

In order that His disciples might not misunderstand, right on the heels of these two powerful parables, Jesus tells them about the judgment day. Those on the left will say, "Lord, when did we ever see You hungry? When did we ever see You naked? When did we ever see You poor? When did we ever see You in prison? When did we ever see You a stranger?" Jesus says, "As much as you did not do it unto the least of these, you didn't do it unto Me."

A child needs love; he needs teaching about Jesus; he needs care; he needs spiritual security; he needs to know God; he needs to learn to feel the presence of God.

It is a powerful lesson. I'm thankful for the benevolent program here, but it is not enough. It is too little, too late. It must be expanded. I'm not fussing. I thank God for these little children's homes, six of them. I tell you one thing; if any of you die today, you can mark this down: If we pillow our head in death, we are a thousand times more ready to meet God because for the last three years 92 little children have received a home. I don't mean just food and clothing; that is just about 20 percent of it. A child needs love; he needs teaching about Jesus; he needs care; he needs spiritual security; he needs to know God; he needs to learn to feel the presence of God. Those children have all that.

I'm thankful today for our furniture program. Did you know that last year our furniture truck worked 400 cases? Did you know that the elders decided Wednesday night we are going to build a warehouse? Our retired men have been saying that they need a warehouse. When you get new furniture, you call Uncle Joe Pharris, and he comes and gets your old furniture. Our retired men polish it up, and we give it to the poor. We are going to build a warehouse right up here on the back of the first lot that we own. We may have to move it someday, but you can take these buildings down and move them.

Do you know what happened yesterday? Within three blocks of this building, there was a little 8-year-old girl sleeping on the floor. She didn't have a bed. One of our elders — I don't want to call his name, but his initials are Roy Holt — and one of our other men, whose initials are Uncle Joe Pharris, took her a bed. That little girl, who lives within three blocks of the largest church of Christ on earth, doesn't have to sleep on the floor. She slept on a bed last night, thank God.

I'm thankful for our food room. Dr. Pettus' class gave us a shower that nearly filled that food room. I'm thankful for it. We need to buy Brother Perry Underwood a truck. It is a shame that a retired man gives his time free of charge and then has to use his own car and his own gas. Maybe some car dealer in this audience will give us a new car? Let's put on it — Food Room: Church of Christ, Madison, Tennessee. Then why don't some of you good brethren who run a service station service it for us free?

I'm thankful for the women who give five days a week to sew for little children. But, dearly beloved, we are not doing half enough. This church could do twice what it is doing, and what a blessing we would be. How we need a generation among churches of Christ to lead us out of the wilderness of criticism, out of the wilderness of littleness, out of the wilderness of do-nothingness. Here is a group of people who claim to be the church that Jesus built, and they are not spending as much money for the poor as they are to feed their cat. How God needs a church in our age that loves the poor and the lowly and the downtrodden and will lead us out in a great work for the lowly.

Dearly beloved, this nation of ours has just experienced what I think is one of the darkest pages in all of its history. No nation can long endure or tolerate what we saw in Los Angeles a few days ago: 2,000 fires deliberately set to people's property; 36 people killed; 700 wounded; over $200 million destroyed in looting and shooting. Such is civil war and insurrection. There isn't anything anybody can say that can justify it, and our leaders had better speak out, and they better speak clear if they don't want this nation to come apart at the seams.

Dearly beloved, there is another side to that coin. What I'm going to say is not very pleasant, but I challenge you to think about it. I know one thing: the message will please the Lord Jesus. If it doesn't please you, that's all right. What have the religious people, what have the churches, done for the poor in the inner city? Not only nondenominational churches of Christ, but what have the denominational churches done? What has Christendom done?

I'll tell you what we have done. For all practical purposes: nothing! When the poor move in, we move out. We don't want to get our hands dirty. So in the inner city they live in poverty, unspeakable poverty on some occasions. Oh, how those little children need to know about Jesus. How they need to feel the hand of someone clean who cares. But what have we done? We have moved out, and we have worshiped in our big, fine buildings with wall-to-wall carpet and air conditioning, ridden in our nice cars, lived in our nice homes, wrung our hands and said: "Oh, those terrible people down in the slums." We haven't turned our hands to help them. What would have happened in that district in Los Angeles if the churches of Christ had gone in and given a little time and love and care and teaching to the little children?

How God needs a church in our age that loves the poor and the lowly and the downtrodden and will lead us out in a great work for the lowly.

There are two places in the United States of America where a little bit has been done that I want to tell you about this morning. One is in Nashville, Tennessee, on the corner of Second Avenue and Lindsley. They call it the Youth Hobby Shop. I don't care whether you call it a service center or Sunday school center or a youth shop or what, but here is what they have done. Nearby is a housing project with poor children in it. Some of them have never seen their daddy, and some of them don't even know who their daddy is. Sometimes dad is in the "pen" and mother is making a few dollars a week at some little cafe, just trying to keep body and soul together. They are underprivileged, undertaught and poor, but

now the young people have a place to go. Every afternoon they go to the Youth Hobby Shop where Brother
and Sister Peltier are there. Between 100 and 150
children come. On one side they have a beauty parlor
where Sister Peltier teaches little girls how to wash
their hair and such. Beside that is a little woodwork-
ing shop to teach those boys to do something with
their hands. Over here is a little craft shop. Back of it
is a little chapel. They come there at night, and they
will play and learn. They have a place to play with
supervision. A college student who worked there
reported one little boy said, "You will have to referee.
You know in the streets we always fight when we
don't have a referee. We can't play without a referee."
They come, and the little girls play here and the boys
there. Before they go home, they come in the chapel
and Brother Peltier says, "Now I want us to pray."
And they will pray and they will sing and they will
talk about Jesus. That is precious and wonderful.
There is not a single place like this in East
Nashville. The only one we have is over there.

The next place I want to tell you about is the House
of the Carpenter. I'm going to see it in Boston two
weeks from tomorrow. They just rented a cheap, little
storefront. College and senior high boys and girls
have gone into the slums, and they are teaching
some kids there. Some of them come in and can't
pass arithmetic, so students help them with that.
Then before they go, they tell the children from the
slums about Jesus and they talk about the Word of
God. Isn't that wonderful?

You know, many times in the church of Christ we
have acted like what our young people need is a

glass of lemonade and a cookie. Our young people do not need a glass of lemonade and a cookie. They have been coddled and entertained too much now. What they need is a challenge. If a boy 18 years is big enough to fight and die for his country, he is big enough to witness for Jesus. He is big enough to do something to help the poor and the under-privileged kids. What our young people need is a challenge. I don't like this expression "our young people are the church of tomorrow." That is not true. Our young people are the church of today. Those who are 18, 19, 20 and in their early 20s — they are the church of today. They need to be busy on the firing line for Jesus.

You know what I would love to see that would thrill my soul? I'd almost give the shirt off of my wife's back to see it. I'd like to see this Madison church select the poorest, most underprivileged area in East Nashville, probably a housing project, and rent a little hall or building and let our people in their late teens and early 20s go there every day to give some time to the children in the area and tell them about Jesus. Take a bus on Sunday morning, and bring them out here to Sunday school. Bring them out here in the summer; take them to Valley View camp and wade the creek with them; sit on a log with them and talk about Jesus.

When I came through Chicago yesterday, I read in a newspaper where 22,000 poor children in Chicago had just graduated from Head Start school. One teacher was telling about what an experience it was. She said many of them had never seen a toy. Can you imagine that a child 5 years old had never seen a toy, had never been over three blocks away from home, had never seen the city of Chicago, had never even been close to a skyscraper, living in that great city?

A member of the church told me that he went into a two-room apartment one time in Washington, D.C., and 16 people were sleeping like cordwood on the floor. I want to ask you today, dearly beloved, and I ask myself: "Suppose I had been born and reared in a situation like that? Suppose, when I was 5 years of age I had never seen my daddy, that I didn't even know who he was. What if I never had a toy I could call my own? I was surrounded by vice and crime. I never felt the touch of a tender hand that was pure and clean. Nobody ever talked to me about Jesus and told me the sweet story and how good it was to live right. Where do you think I would be today?" I don't know. I might well be behind prison bars.

Dearly beloved, the churches of America have met in their big, fine buildings, with their wall-to-wall carpets and their luxury, and they have preached the horns off a brass billy goat — and they haven't turned their hands to minister and serve the poor and the lowly and the downtrodden. Yet Jesus says that at the judgment day He is going to ask us, "What about the stranger? What about the person in prison?"

Last Sunday this church preached at the state prison. Some of our young people went to the prison for women and some went to the prison farm and some went to the workhouse. Yes, there will be Sunday school this afternoon at 2 o'clock at the county workhouse. Some went to the city jail across from the courthouse. In every hospital in this town, somebody went from the Madison Church last Sunday to minister to the sick. That is pure religion; that is undefiled religion; that is a religion that will get us ready to live on earth and ready to live in heaven.

Our young people are the church of today. ... They need to be busy on the firing line for Jesus.

As we build this gigantic auditorium, let us not for one second place the emphasis on this building. It is only sticks and stones and steel. What I want and what you want and what we must have is a greater program for Christ: a greater teaching program, a greater mission program, and a greater and better program of benevolent work. I hope to see the time that we have two or three furniture trucks; two or three food trucks; and every young person in this Sunday school going out every week and ministering to the poor and the lowly and sharing His blessings with those who do not have it. This will prepare us to live in heaven.

The judgment day is coming, and a lot of people on the right side are going to be surprised and say, "Lord, when did we ever see You naked? When did we ever see You hungry? When did we ever see You a stranger? When did we ever see You in prison?" He'll reply, "As much as you did it to the poorest, humblest, weakest of My creatures, you did it unto Me. Come, blessed of My father, inherit the place prepared for you from the foundation of the world."

I want to hear that someday, and I want you to hear it too. If you are not a Christian today, will you believe in Jesus? Will you confess Jesus? Will you be baptized into Jesus, and then will you help us in inaugurating and carrying on a program for the poor in the name of Jesus that will bring renown to the honor and glory of Jesus and will encourage others to get busy for Jesus? Would you do it?

∾

Madison Church of Christ
Madison, Tennessee
1972

The Great Commission

I love the Great Commission. It is the marching orders of the church. "Go ye therefore, and teach all nations, baptizing them into the name of the Father, and of the Son, and of the Holy Ghost: Teaching them to observe all things whatsoever I have commanded you: and, lo, I am with you alway, even unto the end of the world" (Matthew 28:19-20). I couldn't think of a greater, more significant passage in all of the Bible. It gives marching orders of the church of our Lord.

There are three points I want to make in this sermon on the Great Commission. First is that Madison must continue to plan ahead with faith and vision.

The Lord Jesus has taught us the power of setting goals. I am still unable to understand the prejudice of people who do not set goals. Our Lord Jesus, with a handful of men, not a one of them with a college degree, set the greatest goal the world has ever known. He said, "I want you to go to all the world."

Here they were without a jet airplane, without an automobile, with just crudely made ships and donkeys and walking. Yet He says, "I want you to go to all the world." Not just the Mediterranean world, not just the continent, but into all the world. You can't think bigger than that. You can't climb higher than that. You can't set a bigger goal than that.

God said that he wanted the Good News taken to every creature. Not just the Jews. Not just one ethnic group. Don't you get a little weary about all this talk about ethnic groups? Wouldn't it be wonderful if the country could be like we are here at Madison? We don't believe in "us" and "them." We don't even talk of our young people as "them" and the rest of us as "us." We are all in the same boat. We are partners. We are brothers and sisters in the Lord.

And so Jesus says in Mark 16:15, "Go ye into all the world, and preach the gospel to every creature." What a marvelous goal! I want our young people to set goals. I want all of us to set goals, and I want us to remember that goals keep us stretching farther.

What I love about this text is that there is no room for boredom. There is no room for stagnation. There is no room for deadness. Our Lord gave us a goal that will always keep us reaching and growing and stretching until the Gospel is taken into all the world, every creature confesses the name of Jesus, every knee bows, and every tongue confesses. The great tragedy of the local church is that sometimes we spend all of our time only keeping house, taking care of current business. But by the grace of God, we have always planned and must continue to plan ahead with faith and vision.

I love the story that happened in Lawrence County years ago when an old preacher came to hold a meeting in one of the rural areas. He got there on Saturday, which was the custom in those days. The preacher would get there a day early because the transportation was not like it is today. When he got there, the brethren were out in the creek branch damming it up. He said, "Well, I never saw anything like this before. You must think we are going to baptize somebody." The brethren said, "Well, that is up to the Lord. We just always do our part, and we find that God is able to take care of His." The meeting started the next day, and they baptized 45 people. We need to dam up the creek.

The great tragedy of the local church is that sometimes we spend all of our time only keeping house, taking care of current business.

The truth of it is the church cannot coast. When a church lives in the past, instead of thanking God for the blessings today and planning ahead, it is an old dead church. There isn't any such thing as coasting in the work of the Lord. Oh, I know that sometimes we are tempted to say, "Well, let's coast." There is an element of pleasure in coasting. I remember riding a bicycle to the top of Rockdale Hill in southern Middle Tennessee. Then we would coast down that hill for about three miles. We went around those curves, which was such fun. But we knew every second we were going down hill that before we could come home we had to turn around and climb that hill. I want to tell you one thing: It was a tough climb.

The tragedy of coasting is that it is never up. It is always down. It is never for the better. It is always for the worse. It is buying a little time here and paying it back with tremendous effort. The tragedy of coasting is that the momentum picks up the longer you coast until you've had it.

I know a church not many miles from here that had reached a marvelous point. They had everything — talent, money, love, power — everything except the desire to climb ahead with faith and vision. So they began to coast. But what they are finding is that the coasting is downhill, and the momentum is picking up. Everything now is in such a state that the leadership is in panic. They say, "If we coast the next five years as much as we have in the last, there is not going to be anybody here left to coast."

Coasting is always down hill. It takes no effort. It is a mockery. It promises such ease. The preacher doesn't get fired coasting. Nobody gets upset coasting. We struggle going uphill. We struggle swimming against the tide. But it is the only way of growth. So I say first of all today, let's continue to plan ahead with great faith and vision.

This church must always be a young church in spirit. I hope that the life of the late J.L. Hunter, who was an elder here for many years, will inspire us in this respect. When Brother Hunter was 83, he was out in the yard planning to build another room on his house. He never talked to me about dying. He talked to me about living. He was always young. He was always looking ahead, and he died in the zenith

of his life. God took him after all those years of zest
and enthusiasm and usefulness. He was there at
every elders' meeting. You would have thought he
was 23 years old I think in many respects maybe he
was the youngest of us all.

The second thing I want to mention as we talk
about planning ahead for the coming years is I hope
we will continue to allow the Scriptures to sustain
us and bring us a great inspiration in this church.
There are three stories in the Bible that have served
as a beacon light to this church. I call your attention
to them today as we look ahead.

One, is the Old Testament story of three Hebrew
children. The Old Testament is of God. You know,
occasionally we think we are so smart, and we say,
"Well, I'll tell you: I don't know about these
Scriptures in the Old Testament." Yet Paul says,
"For whatsoever things were written aforetime were
written for our learning, that we through patience
and comfort of the scriptures might have hope"
(Romans 15:4).

Now occasionally someone will pick out, for example, the story of Jonah in the belly of the great fish
for three days, and say, "Oh, that is just terrible."
Well, it is if somebody doesn't have any faith. But if
you believe that the United States government can
make a mechanical fish [submarine] that will swal-
low a hundred men and keep them down a hundred
days, you don't have any trouble believing that the
God of heaven can keep one man down for three
days. He wasn't down just three days for nothing.
That event was the forerunner of the greatest event
to ever happen on earth, which is the resurrection of

our Lord, who was in the heart of the earth for three days as Jonah was in the belly of that great fish.

You remember the story about the three Hebrew boys in Daniel 3. They were told: "You must to fall down and worship something else. This Jehovah won't do. Almighty God won't do." Those who didn't bow to an idol were to be thrown in a fiery furnace. So they said, "If it be so, our God whom we serve is able to deliver us from the burning fiery furnace, and he will deliver us out of thine hand, O king" (Daniel 3:17). The point of it is, they faced such crisis with their great faith. Our God is able. Little men are fearful. Big men are men of faith. I don't know that these three Hebrew children had much education or much prestige or much power, but I know one thing: They were mighty men of faith when they said, "Our God is able."

Our God is able. Little men are fearful. Big men are men of faith.

The second instance that has helped us so much is the instruction of our Lord to Peter, James and John after they had fished all night in the Sea of Galilee (Luke 5:1-11). The beautiful, marvelous sea, so clear and cool. The fish are so tasty, even until this good day. Now, they were pros at fishing. The Lord said, "Launch out a little deeper. Go on out a little deeper. Launch out into the deep." They answered, "Well, Lord, we will do it if You bid it, but it won't do any good." They had the defeatist attitude that has damned churches all over this world: "It won't do any good. It won't work here. We are pros. We know it

won't work." Jesus said, "Launch out into the deep."
When they launched out into the deep, they had a
catch that was unbelievable. So it is in the spiritual
world until this good day. What a tragedy it would
have been if we here at Madison had not launched
out into the deep. In the years ahead, I hope this little incident on the Sea of Galilee will inspire us.

The third scripture that has served as a great
source of inspiration and will sustain us in the days
ahead is the instruction of the apostle Paul to "keep
the unity of the Spirit in the bond of peace"
(Ephesians 4:3). This church is firmly committed to
doing that.

These are great scriptures. They are just as relevant and up to date and needed today as ever. They
are all right in the '70s. They are all right in the
'80s. They are all right in the '90s. Until the Lord
comes again, there won't be anything wrong with
these scriptures. They will be just as powerful and
wonderful. Let us continue.

The third thing I want to mention as we anticipate
the future is I hope that we will look to the future
with great enthusiasm and great zest. Madison is a
young church — young in spirit. Our old people are
young in spirit, and our young people are wise above
their years. As I look ahead with you today, I see
three things I hope we can look forward to with
enthusiasm and zest.

I believe the greatest and most urgent need at the
Madison Church is in the realm of our educational
program, our Sunday school. I hope that you will
help me and we will all work together to make next
year the greatest year of Bible teaching that we

have ever known. Brother C.J. Garner is coming home in a few weeks, and he will work with us full time here with our bus ministry. I know the bus committee is thrilled to have C.J. Garner. He has a lot of enthusiasm and zest, and he believes in the Sunday school as much as any man in America. That is wonderful. I'm hoping and praying that at Operation Forward, our planning session, somebody will recommend an expansion for our educational facility. The truth of it is, at Madison we have reached the saturation point in Sunday school. We have reached it twice, and I don't think another Sunday school is practical. Four services on Sunday is all she wrote, and I think we would be foolish to think we can work in another one. I have never seen a church in my life that uses its facilities seven days and seven nights a week like we do. Somehow we have got to make room.

I wish and pray that some of our financial wizards who work in figures every day will come up with something to help us. God has been good. We could have a three-story annex like where the white cottage is and a playground, and we could take care of our preschool, nursery and first grade. You know we have 500 kids in our Sunday school who have not started to school. We used to have five grades in a department, then four, then three, and now we have two. What we really need is one. We could have facilities for a department for every year at least through age seventeen. It would do wonders for this Sunday school.

I pray that we can soon complete our camp at Valley View. We have such a wonderful program in the summer of teaching the Bible. We teach as much

Bible in two weeks at camp as an average Sunday school can teach in a year. Young people are so precious, and they won't wait. The tragedy is that you can't sit around and wait. The child who is 6 today will be 16 in 10 years, and it will be too late. I think our most urgent need is the Sunday school.

I think the second need, and I believe we are ready for it, is an increase in our mission program. I think we can do this in two ways. The mission committee is recommending that we go to one of the big cities in the Northeast, buy land, build a home that will take care of homeless children. We'll get a couple of preachers, let the church meet in the basement, and grow a church in a new area. The committee has thought about it for years and the elders have said to go ahead and investigate. We believe that this may be one of the most effective ways of reaching the lost.

I do believe the time has come when talk without action will lose our young people by the thousands.

I am hoping our mission emphasis can increase also with the growing of our television program because, make no mistake about it, this television ministry is mission work. We are going through the airways to the homes of thousands of people. We are developing them through Bible correspondence courses. We are getting into homes that we couldn't dream of getting in, not even by knocking on doors. We have now a worldwide door open through the Armed Services. Now I pray that our mission work may continue. I hope we can build a church in a city and see it self-supported. I hope that God's providence will stay with us to be in every market in the United States of America, showing that Christian people are happy, the Bible is relevant, and Christ is great and needed today.

Christian people are happy, the Bible is relevant, and Christ is great and needed today.

Finally, let us not lose sight of our interest in pure and undefiled religion. Thank God for the children. Thank God for Meals on Wheels. Thank God for the food room. Thank God for the furniture room. Thank God for the Golden Age Village. We have a wonderful benevolent program. Maybe we have done more preaching with more emphasis on helping the poor, lowly, downtrodden and the homeless. But I'm convinced it has brought us the smile of God, the help of Jesus, and also the help of hundreds of you who want to have a part in something that is real, pure religion. I do believe the time has come when talk without action will lose our young people by the thousands. They are leaving organized religion in this country by the thousands, and I think one reason is they do not see a relevancy. They don't see the local church feeding the hungry and helping the homeless, the poor and the lowly, and the downtrodden. They don't see a practice of a pure and undefiled religion. They say, "What is all this preaching? We've got to get out there where the action is. Let us have a little practice."

In closing, I want to urge us to continue. Let us stay young in spirit. Let us always live today and plan ahead for tomorrow with faith and vision. Let us always dream dreams. Let us always strive for one more soul. God grant that this church may always struggle, strive, plan and want one more. God grant that the time never comes when we feel like we have arrived, when we think we have enough, or when one more soul is not precious. For Jesus said to leave the 99 and go after the one (Matthew 18:12-14). We are interested in you. Will you come today?

∾

Madison Church of Christ
Madison, Tennessee
October 8, 1972

I believe in the deity of Christ;
the brotherhood of man; the
fatherhood of God; the church of
our Lord; the plan of salvation.

— *Ira North*